Intimate Communities of Hate

Social media has fundamentally transformed political life, driving a surge in far-right extremism. In recent years, radical anti-democratic ideologies have entered into the political mainstream, fueled by energy from extreme online environments. But why do far-right extremist movements seem to thrive so well on social media platforms? What takes place within the fringe online spaces that seem to function as incubators for violent extremists? To answer these questions, this book goes inside the "murder capital of the racist Internet", examining 20 years of conversations on Stormfront.org. Using a combination of computational text analysis and close reading, we seek a deeper understanding of the emotional and social effects of being part of an extremist community. We lay the foundation of a new way of understanding online extremism, building on the tradition of Émile Durkheim and Randall Collins. We find that online radicalization is not merely an effect of repeated one-sided arguments, as suggested by metaphors such as "echo chambers". Instead, social media politics can be better understood through Durkheim's concept of *rituals*: moments of shared attention and emotion that create emotional energy and a sense of intersubjectivity, weaving from participants a political tribe – united, energized, and poised to act.

Anton Törnberg is an Associate Professor of Sociology at the University of Gothenburg, Sweden. His primary research interests center on online far-right movements, with a special emphasis on online radicalization processes. He is currently doing research on the links between right-wing violence and social media, as well as the spread of conspiracy theories and climate denialism.

Petter Törnberg is an Assistant Professor in Computational Social Science at the University of Amsterdam and an Associate Professor in Complex Systems at Chalmers University of Technology. His research focuses on the intersection between AI, social media, and politics, using computational methods to examine online polarization and radicalization.

Routledge Studies in Political Sociology

This series presents the latest research in political sociology. It welcomes both theoretical and empirical studies that pay close attention to the dynamics of power, popular protest, and social movements, as well as work that engages in debates surrounding globalization, democracy, and political economy.

Titles in this series

Intimate Communities of Hate

Why Social Media Fuels Far-Right
Extremism

Anton Törnberg and Petter Törnberg

Routledge
Taylor & Francis Group

LONDON AND NEW YORK

First published 2024
by Routledge
4 Park Square, Milton Park, Abingdon, Oxon OX14 4RN

and by Routledge
605 Third Avenue, New York, NY 10158

Routledge is an imprint of the Taylor & Francis Group, an informa business

© 2024 Anton Törnberg and Petter Törnberg

British Library Cataloguing-in-Publication Data
A catalogue record for this book is available from the British Library

Library of Congress Cataloging-in-Publication Data
Names: Törnberg, Anton, author. | Törnberg, Petter, author.
Title: Intimate communities of hate : why social media fuels far-right extremism / Anton Törnberg and Petter Törnberg.
Description: Abingdon, Oxon ; New York, NY : Routledge, 2024. |
Series: Routledge studies in political sociology | Includes bibliographical references and index.
Identifiers: LCCN 2023047480 (print) | LCCN 2023047481 (ebook) |
ISBN 9780367622039 (hardback) | ISBN 9780367622008 (paperback) |
ISBN 9781003108344 (ebook)
Subjects: LCSH: Social media--Political aspects. | Radicalization. | Right-wing extremists. | Radicalism in mass media.
Classification: LCC HM742 .T67 2024 (print) | LCC HM742 (ebook) |
DDC 302.23/1--dc23/eng/20231019
LC record available at https://lccn.loc.gov/2023047480
LC ebook record available at https://lccn.loc.gov/2023047481

ISBN: 978-0-367-62203-9 (hbk)
ISBN: 978-0-367-62200-8 (pbk)
ISBN: 978-1-003-10834-4 (ebk)

DOI: 10.4324/9781003108344

Typeset in Times New Roman
by KnowledgeWorks Global Ltd.

To juju, lolo, Cleo and Jack.

Contents

Prologue

April 1981, New Orleans. Don Black is about to board the ship *Mañana*. Don is ex-military and has been a Grand Dragon of the Alabama Knights of the Ku Klux Klan. Some years prior, he led robed Klansmen on marches through Birmingham. But now he is on a different mission. Mañana is loaded with a cache of automatic weapons, ten 12-gauge shotguns, dynamite, ammunition, a Nazi flag, bottles of Jack Daniels, and a band of hardened mercenaries. They are headed for the island country of Dominica – most known today as the island where Johnny Depp sailed in the *Pirates of the Caribbean*. The group is planning to invade the island and stage a military coup to oust its Black-run government and establish a White neo-Nazi state.

But before Mañana can cast off, 34 armed federal agents who have been watching the would-be invaders' every move through electronic surveillance move in. Don Black is arrested and sentenced to three years in prison for violating the US Neutrality Act, prohibiting private citizens from invading sovereign nations.

While this meant the end for the ragtag band of neo-Nazis' dreams of Caribbean island rule, the arrest of Don Black became the beginning of something even more consequential. Something with far-reaching and deadly consequences.

In prison, Black decided to take classes in computer programming.

As a former Grand Dragon, Don Black was no newcomer to recruiting and mobilizing, and he quickly saw the potential of emerging information technology such as the Internet. "I'm tired of the Jewish monopoly in media and entertainment, and I'm working an alternative. The Internet offers unprecedented opportunities", Black said in an interview in the mid-90s. "The Internet offers us the opportunity to recruit people from all over society. People who hold positions of power, who work within the system but are tired of it, and who want to change things".

Don Black would use his new-found programming skills to create an online forum launched in March 1995. This forum was to grow into one of the most influential far-right websites of the first decades of the Internet – referred to by the Guardian as "the murder capital of the Internet" for its connection to many violent attacks over a decades-long surge of far-right terrorism. Under its tagline *WHITE PRIDE WORLD WIDE*, it was to epitomize the Internet's role in a new wave of far-right extremism centered around the use of new digital media technology.

The forum was *Stormfront.org*. This book will tell the story of Stormfront and what it can teach us about the broader question of how the Internet has transformed far-right movements and extremist radicalization. How do we understand the role of fringe online spaces like Stormfront in relation to extremist movements? How do these spaces affect the political lives of their members? How do they become part of extremist radicalization – as members come to construct a shared worldview, seemingly severed from both reality and society at large? How do these spaces emotionally charge their members to be ready to commit violent acts?

These are the questions that will guide us as we go inside a white power echo chamber.

Introduction

Stormfront grew rapidly after its inception. By the early 2000s, the forum was described in an article in USA Today as "the most visited white supremacist site on the net" (McKelvey, 2001). The number of registered members rose from 5,000 in 2002 to 52,566 in 2005. Among these members were prominent white supremacists, such as Thom Robb, the founder of National States Rights Party Ed Fields, and former KKK leader David Duke, who had collaborated with Don Black in organizing the failed invasion of Dominica. In 2005, Stormfront ranked among the top 1% of internet sites in terms of visitors. The community is also distinguished by its remarkable longevity: while the internet went through waves of transformation – the Dot-Net boom of the early 2000, Web 2.0, and the emergence of social media – Stormfront remained a fixed point.

In the period when Stormfront emerged, the internet was viewed with hopeful anticipation. Scholars and the public alike saw the internet as bringing a democratization of public debate (Castells, 2008; Perry, 1996). It removed the gatekeepers – editors and publishers, predominantly well-off white men – who had in previous era had sole discretion over what was deemed publishable (McCombs, Shaw & Weaver, 1997; McQuail, 1987). By allowing anyone to participate in discussions, the internet democratized access to the public sphere, thus shifting the majority from passive consumption to active participation (Jenkins, 2006). Feminist scholars argued that it would foster a color- and gender-blind public sphere by concealing the identity of our interlocutors and enabling a more fluid relationship to our identities (Butler, 2002; Haraway, 1985; Rodino, 1997). The early internet was thus largely associated with progressive movements, emphasizing its potential as a liberating force in an era marked by the end of the Cold War – synonymous with progress in minority rights, a spirit of openness, and a vision of a unified world.

However, the politics of both the internet and the prevalent political climate were on the precipice of a dramatic shift. The growth of Stormfront in the 2000s coincided with the rise of the far right in much of the Western world, seen in the electoral successes of far-right political parties,

DOI: 10.4324/9781003108344-1

anti-immigrant rhetoric entering the political mainstream and in nationalist street protests. Among the more gruesome expressions of its ascendance is a dramatic increase in far-right violence and terror attacks. According to the Institute for Economics & Peace's (2019) Global Terrorism Index, the last few years alone have seen a 320% surge in far-right terrorism in the West – the vast majority carried out by individuals who lack formal affiliation with any organization.

The recent surge in extremism differs from previous waves of right-wing extremism in that it is facilitated, mobilized, and orchestrated through social media. Social media platforms have become valuable tools for far-right movements and activists, providing efficient means of mobilizing (Mundt, Ross & Burnett, 2018), spreading their hateful messages (Castaño-Pulgarín et al., 2021; Farkas, Schou & Neumayer, 2017; Ganesh, 2020), recruiting members (Ekman, 2018), creating networks and coalitions (Caiani, 2018; Caiani, Della Porta & Wagemann, 2012; Veilleux-Lepage & Archambault, 2019), and organizing street protests (Liang & Cross, 2020; Miller & Graves, 2020). However, online spaces not only serve as tools for these movements but have also been shown to transform the very nature of the movements – functioning as a form of sanctuary where members can develop a sense of collective identity and construct counter-narratives to mainstream ideas (Bowman-Grieve, 2009; Jasser et al., 2021; Koster & Houtman, 2008; Perry & Scrivens, 2016; Simi & Futrell, 2006, 2015). Social media has, in this sense, become inextricably intertwined with the process of radicalization.

Emphasizing the role of social media as having become part of the formation and recruitment of extremist communities inherently challenges the conventional understanding of radicalization. Much of the early literature framed radicalization as something that is *done to* people. These perspectives either focused on individual-centric explanations, such as elusive "terrorist personality" (Sageman, 2004, 2008), or systemic social grievances like economic disparity, inadequate education, or feelings of alienation from society. However, empirical evidence supporting these claims is sparse (Agnew, 2010; Della Porta, 1995). Following McDonald (2018), it may instead be more productive to view radicalization as a relational and processual phenomenon – "something produced by active participants, attempting to make sense of themselves and their world." (p. 27). As this book will argue, to understand contemporary far-right radicalization, we need to examine how social media offers technological affordances that aid processes of socialization, in which participants gradually adopt the identities, emotions, and interpretations of a far-right community (Marwick, Clancy & Furl, 2022). While social media has transformed society and politics in general, we will argue that it has been particularly transformative of extremist movements – creating altogether new dynamics, pathways, and expressions of radicalization (Binder & Kenyon, 2022; Sageman, 2008; Whittaker, 2022). While historically, radicalization occurred primarily through recruitment into formal organizations, this process has increasingly migrated to the online sphere, with significant implications (Khader, 2016; Koehler, 2014; Valentini, Lorusso & Stephan, 2020).

Firstly, this transformation has implicated a marked shift towards the role of language and discourse in radicalization. In the past, face-to-face encounters, physical gatherings like street protests and white power concerts, and sub-cultural attires like t-shirts and even the color of shoelaces played significant roles in constructing and symbolizing belonging, community, and dedication to extremist communities. In the context of online radicalization, these processes now seem to occur exclusively in the discursive realm: community, belonging, and identities are constructed through meetings in online spaces and symbolized through internal discourses and cultures where memes, jargon, images, and even specific words function as emblems and evidence of group membership. In this regard, radicalization processes now primarily unfold through linguistic processes.

Secondly, digitalization has driven the decentralization of extremist movements, often resulting in a lack of explicit leadership. In conventional formal movements, ideology and framing processes are primarily driven by movement leadership, who defined and diagnosed the problem, provided potential solutions, and suggested courses of action (Benford, 1997; Benford & Snow, 2000). Ideologies and collective action frames were thus typically constructed and disseminated in a top-down process. However, we now see the emergence of a more fragmentary type of extremist organization and radicalization driven by social media users themselves. Conventional frames tended to be relatively consistent and integrated packages, polished to avoid contradictions and strategically designed to garner the support of politicians and to attract sympathizers. In stark contrast, the construction of ideology and movement framing are now fragmented processes by and for movement actors.

As an effect of this intertwinement between social media and extremist communities, far-right extremism has become more unpredictable and, in many ways, more dangerous. Scholars have described the emergence of "stochastic terrorism", which posits that social media discussions can incite random actors to carry out violent or terrorist acts that are statistically predicable, even though the timing and specific targets of these attacks remain unpredictable (Hamm & Spaaij, 2017; Miller-Idriss, 2022; Tsesis, 2017). Both experimental evidence and observational studies have found that passive and, particularly, active exposure to radical online content increases both support for and involvement in political violence (Hassan et al., 2018; Karell et al., 2023; Müller & Schwarz, 2020a, 2020b; Wolfowicz, Hasisi & Weisburd, 2022).

While organizations enabled the extremist and violent movements of the past, they also provided contextual constraints and relational ties that – for better or worse – disciplined political action and guided participants toward repertoires geared at the strategic pursuit of longer-term goals, such as organization-building or collective manifestations (Raymond, 1999; Shirky, 2008; Weinberger, 2007). As a result, radicalized individuals unaffiliated with formal organizations tend to pose greater risks. Data on far-right attacks in Europe from 1990 to 2021 support this notion, showing that the majority of fatal attacks during this period were carried out by lone actors. In contrast, non-fatal attacks were predominantly executed by autonomous cells, informal groups, organized groups, and affiliated members (Ravndal, 2016, 2018).

While social media has become intertwined with contemporary extremist movements, fundamentally shaping their form and expression, the mechanisms through which social media enable radicalization remain poorly understood. Within media and communication studies, as well as in public discourse, the notion of "echo chambers" has become a dominant explanation for online radicalization (Pariser, 2011; Sunstein, 2002, 2008). This notion suggests that online spaces isolate individuals from opposing viewpoints and that this leads to more extreme opinions. Public sphere theorists have long argued that individuals coming together with diverse ideas and perspectives is central to democracy, as it enables working out disagreements and forming a "public" through rational deliberation. However, when such deliberation takes place in homogeneous spaces where individuals are exposed only to one-sided content, this is instead said to result in extreme political views that potentially prime participants to engage in violent action (McPherson, Smith-Lovin & Cook, 2001; Sunstein, 2007). The accompanying notion of "filter bubbles" suggests that these effects are further reinforced by algorithmic personalization that automatically selects content based on the viewers' preferences while hiding opposing views and perspectives. Ultimately, this leads to that users may "self-radicalize" by falling into online "rabbit holes" and emerge as "lone-wolf" terrorists.

The echo chamber hypothesis lies as an explicit or implicit foundation of much of the current paradigm of online radicalization and polarization research, shaping not only the methods used but also the view on the nature of phenomena such as social media, radicalization, and politics. This paradigm views political life as chiefly a question of opinions and issue positions, and social media as a space for debate and the exchange of rational arguments. Although the processing taking place inside echo chambers may appear anything but "rational", this perspective treats radical politics as a property of individuals and political views as stemming from rational understanding and interpretation of information and knowledge presented in arguments. Social media is thus presumed to spur radicalization and polarization by facilitating and accelerating isolation and keeping groups separate from each other.

The result has been a research paradigm seeking to examine the structure of interaction on media platforms, that is, who talks with whom – while largely disregarding the content and meaning of the messages thus exchanged. As a result, the paradigm has drawn extensively on quantitative methods such as Social Network Analysis and measurements such as homophily or clustering as the operationalization of echo chambers, examining the networks constituted by how individuals on social media retweet, mention, or follow one another.

However, the notion of echo chambers as the prime driver behind radicalization and polarization has been questioned by growing empirical evidence. There are two chief problems with the hypothesis.

First, studies show that online radical groups tend to be neither isolated nor homogenous. In fact, substantial empirical evidence demonstrates that although political information often circulates within specific channels and groups, groups also communicate with each other, allowing arguments and worldviews to permeate various environments (Bail, 2022; Bail et al., 2018b; Dubois & Blank, 2018; Jungherr, Rivero & Gayo-Avello, 2020). Studies have shown that internet usage can actually contribute to increased heterogeneity of political discussion networks through inadvertent exposure, originating from the internet's capacity to facilitate access to political differences, even when the individuals do not actively seek them.

Numerous studies have shown that engaging with oppositional views is, in fact, a core practice among many online far-right groups and individuals. Despite their hostility towards mainstream media in general, these actors heavily rely on links to mainstream news sites and social media platforms such as YouTube and Twitter in their discussions (Haller & Holt, 2019; Törnberg & Nissen, 2022). This serves to substantiate their viewpoints and to highlight perceived hypocrisy or inconsistencies in their political adversaries' positions (Heft et al., 2021). Consequently, rather than being insulated, closed-off enclaves or echo chambers, where certain opinions and ideas are reinforced in the absence of competing ideas, these groups' activities are more aptly described as a type of "trench warfare" dynamics in that they often raise opposing arguments and engage with competing views (see also Karlsen et al., 2017; Törnberg & Wahlström, 2018). The discussions, are characterized not by isolation and homogeneity but by significant negative and conflictual interaction across political lines. Many "echoes" within these echo chambers are not core beliefs being restated but rather the sound of opposing viewpoints being critiqued, undermined, and marginalized. Consequently, while fringe online communities certainly do exist, they appear to be defined not so much by isolation – but by active conflict (Keuchenius, Törnberg & Uitermark, 2021). Fringe online spaces, in short, cannot be accurately described as homogenous echo chambers, at least not in the sense of being isolated from alternative viewpoints.

Second, the assumption that isolation leads to radicalization, and interaction across the political divide leads to more moderate and informed views has been questioned by empirical research. Empirical studies on counter-radicalization reveal that strategies based on the idea of "popping the bubble" and increasing interaction between opposing groups can actually fuel conflicts and intensify radicalization and polarization (Bélanger et al., 2020; Lewandowsky et al., 2012). For instance, in a study on Twitter users, Chris Bail and colleagues (2018a) exposed 1,200 users to content from the opposite political spectrum over a one-month period. The results showed that Republicans who were exposed to messages from Democrats expressed markedly more conservative views than before. In fact, the more attention they paid to the content, the stronger the effect. Many participants in the study described the experience of stepping outside their echo chamber as an attack upon their identity. Similar results have been observed in relation to de-radicalization strategies, such as "debunking" or "counter-messaging", which aim to correct factual inaccuracies. Studies show that attempts to refute or quash rumors, such as the falsehood that vaccines cause autism, may exacerbate fears among those who believe these rumors, making them even more concerned about vaccinating their children (Berinsky, 2017; Nyhan et al., 2014). Overall, being exposed to alternative viewpoints and perspectives does not necessarily contribute to a better competition of ideas but can also lead to a vicious competition of identities, sharpening the contrast between "us" and "them" (Törnberg, 2022).

As a result of such findings, the echo chamber hypothesis is increasingly viewed by researchers as an intellectual cul-de-sac. This prompts a need to reassess our understanding of the inner working of radical political spaces online and the driving forces behind extreme politics. If it is not the echo chamber mechanism of a feedback loop between isolation and diverging opinions that drive polarization and radicalization, then what is? Why do social media – and fringe digital spaces in particular – seem to breed terrorists and fuel opposition and polarization?

This book will seek to challenge not only the notion of echo chambers but also the broader understanding of media and politics within which this concept is situated. We will propose an alternative framework for understanding both politics and social media. While social media has contributed to a decline in formal organizations and their role in political radicalization, it has not resulted in a decline in the social dimensions of radical movements, as implied by the echo chamber narrative. Radical movements on online media, we will argue, operate not chiefly in the realm of rational arguments and opinions but in the realm of emotion and community.

While research within the echo chamber paradigm has focused chiefly on a view from afar, using Social Network Analysis and quantitative measures of the structure of online interaction, we will take the opposite methodological approach: we will focus on the content of the interaction, and take an in-depth view into what takes place in an extremist online community, and how its members are affected by their participation. Through an empirical deep-dive into the processes at work on Stormfront, we will lay the foundation of a new paradigm of online radicalization research. This perspective sees the roots of radicalization not in rational deliberation, opinions, and arguments but views both politics and social media through a more social lens. We turn from public spheres and rational debate to theories of rituals, emotion, culture, and community.

In this book, we align with a recent approach in the literature, predominantly inspired by the social movement literature, that perceives radicalization as a process of socialization through which a person comes to view themselves as part of a collective that is characterized by an ideology that explicitly advocates for intergroup violence or domination (cf. Della Porta, 2018; Marwick et al., 2022). Community membership emerges through a process where participants begin by watching, lurking around, learning the norms, and gradually internalizing its practices and values. In this view, radicalization is a group effort where strong bonds, emotional ties, and in-group dynamics are central, as individuals are gradually socialized into the group's norms and ideology. While prior perspectives have regarded this socialization as a face-to-face interaction within small, tightly knit, and often secluded social groups (McCauley & Moskalenko, 2008; Sageman, 2004; Wiktorowicz, 2005), this book sets out to examine how social media has created new rooms for these processes. We investigate how online communities, such as Stormfront, can offer important social functions, serving as sources of bonding, perpetuating out-group antagonism, and promoting shared social norms through group pressure and conformity.

From Rationality to Rituals: A Social Theory of Online Politics

As we immersed ourselves in the discussions on Stormfront – the fervent debates over the correct positioning of various ethnic groups within racial hierarchies, the detailed explorations of some fringe Jewish conspiracy theory, and protracted discourses on the supremacy of the Aryan race – it quickly became evident that these forum discussions were not driven by any commonly accepted understanding of rational deliberation. These conversations did not aim to rationally persuade or to lay out arguments. Instead, they seemed to serve a more symbolic end – to show belonging, to prove shared hatred for the other, and to highlight individuals' knowledge within the intricate discursive world of the community. The messages were ways of highlighting similarities and differences to distinguish an "us" separated from a "them".

Rather than rational arguments, the words and stories seemed rather to serve the role of symbolic markers of identity and belonging. Each thread of discussion appeared as a collective moment of shared energy and emotion, binding together the community through constant references to previous discussions and the collective memory of the community – weaving a discursive web of phrases, memes, stories, and internal lingo. To understand the often intimate social life of this community and comprehend how individuals are affected by participating in its online politics, the conventional theories of political debate – stemming from the romanticized imaginaries of the intellectual movements behind the French and American revolution – felt inapt. We thus turned instead to another foundational thinker: Émile Durkheim, the intellectual legacy of the founder of modern sociology, to provide the foundation for a new theory.

At the turn of the 20th century, Emile Durkheim was seeking to understand what holds communities and societies together. He turned to studying Aboriginal tribes and the role of communal gatherings – featuring dancing and rhythmic chanting around the communal campfire – in fostering community cohesion and culture. He found rituals to be at the core of what produces the shared identity of communities.

The artifacts that were part of these rituals became filled with cultural meaning; they came to represent and even contain the community. In the theories that Durkheim constructed through these studies, culture and community identity are inextricably interlinked: a sense of community is woven through storytelling and the articulation of a common worldview. A community is ultimately composed of cultural artifacts and stories, which link the members with the community.

As theorists of identity, such as Polkinghorne (1988), Bruner (1991), and Sarbin (1986) have later elaborated, language and storytelling are thus centrally intertwined with the notion of community and belonging. Language is a form of social and ideological practice that mediates, influences, and even constructs our experiences, identities, and ways of viewing the world. As we adopt the language of a community and absorb its symbols, we change who we are. We construct our life stories using the symbolic resources available to us, creating links between our personal identity and our community. The acquisition of a shared system of discourse is central to socialization and provides the illusion of a coherent and bounded identity by situating the individual in the social. Language is, in short, the stuff of the social world.

Scholars who have examined community stories have found that these are centrally linked to emotions (Collins, 2004; Eyerman, 2004). Rituals allow the communities to process difficult emotions, and stories allow them to make sense of their experiences and their role in the world (Alexander, 2004; Eyerman, 2022). These stories are more than told – they are viscerally felt, as they are intimately entangled with the identity and self-understanding of the participants. When our self-perceptions and the stories that link us to our social communities are threatened or broken, it can result in profound emotional distress or even trauma. These conflicts between our stories and the community that provides our comfort force us to either reject or reexamine our stories. Emotions play a crucial role in community and movement life as they motivate and drive individuals to engage in collective action.

The Durkheimian notion of a ritual thus links together identity, storytelling, and emotions in a single process. These processes are not different from the healthy social processes of community and belonging that are central to all human life: we all need to feel belonging; we all need to make sense of our world. Taking this Durkheimian perspective on political radicalization and extremism suggests that we must understand conflict, violence, and extremism as rooted in normal processes of belonging and community. We can, in other words, not have separate theories for solidarity and conflict: they are two sides of the same coin. Conflict is not the opposite of social cooperation and solidarity; we cannot have a sentimental theory of human beings on one hand and a cynical conflict theory on the other. It is all part of the same process: external conflict can strengthen solidarity within a group, and internal solidarity can intensify external conflict. Our in-group becomes identified with good and what is outside it with evil. This makes violence seem morally right: if we feel completely virtuous, everything we do will be good, whether it is murder, mutilation, or massacre; and correspondingly, if our enemy is completely evil, they deserve what is done to them (Collins, 2012).

Examining Stormfront through this Durkheimian lens allows us to refocus our understanding of radicalization: it is not the result of isolation from opposing arguments, as the echo chamber hypothesis suggests. Instead, online spaces such as Stormfront are distinctly social: the digital equivalent of the communal gatherings where Aboriginals convened over a century ago. These platforms weave, from the fabric of recurrent interaction, a form of digital tribes – with a shared sense of collective identity, a distinct way of understanding the world, and the emotional energy that propels collective action. This perspective redirects our attention from the apparent contents of these discussions – whether Jewish conspiracies or Aryan supremacy – to their *social* meaning: the act of interacting itself. Like in the Aboriginal chanting, the words are less significant than the rhythm, the feeling, and the sense of shared activity. As much as belonging to the realm of argumentation, opinion, and rationality, what takes place on social media is also deeply rooted in the realm of identity, ritual, and symbolism. Through this lens, Stormfront appears less as an echo chamber in which our views are confirmed through repetition but rather conjures images of a modern-day digital campfire: shared social spaces around which we can gather and over time turn from strangers into a community woven through shared moments of storytelling, sensemaking and presence.

Book Structure

To develop this argument, we will go inside the White Power online community Stormfront to examine the social processes shaping the digital social lives of far-right extremists. We have acquired the full dataset of discussions on Stormfront, constituting 10,172,069 posts and 354,574 users, spanning over 20 years of discussion. The Stormfront dataset provides a view into how social media is affecting the political life of individuals – as they come to view themselves as part of the community and begin to construct a shared worldview with common enemies and grievances. Instead of the structural and from-afar view that has characterized much of the research on echo chambers, we focus on questions of meaning-making, emotion, and identity, suggesting a more in-depth approach. By employing a computational pluralist approach, combining computational methods with in-depth qualitative analysis, and drawing upon digital media research and, in particular, social movement theory, we will examine the role that Stormfront played in shaping the movement it incubated.

While few researchers have had ethnographic access to the internal processes of historical extremist communities, we have a complete record of discussions and conversations within the Stormfront community. Such "Big Data" create new opportunities to trace the actions and interactions of individuals, study the processes of socialization, and investigate how the community collectively makes sense of the world. The dataset thus offers unique insights into the "backstage" of social movements, illuminating what social movement scholar Alberto Melucci (1996) has referred to as "latent movement activity". This includes the oft-invisible networks and interactions of the every day: the "cultural laboratories" where alternative values and counter-discourses are generated and negotiated.

By drawing on this unique empirical data source, our aim is to understand what takes place within the fringe digital spaces from which contemporary extremist movements emerge. Why do these spaces breed radical movements? How do they foster political subjects? How do these social media spaces produce a coherent movement from an unseen set of strangers? How do they develop a shared language, culture, and norms? How do we understand the social effects of engaging in online political discussions – how they affect how we view ourselves and our relation to our social world?

Chapter 1 situates Stormfront in the broader academic debate on the public sphere and the relationship between the structure of such spaces and political life. We will look at the history through which social media has been understood and argue for an alternative way to conceptualize social media in general and online spaces such as Stormfront in particular.

Chapter 2 explores the social processes that bring about the emergence of a political subject by elaborating a Durkheimian approach to online radicalization. This chapter focuses on the three central components of the social process – identity, emotion, and worldview – and draws on the works of Emile Durkheim and Randall Collins. This lays the theoretical groundwork for the empirical explorations in Chapters 5, 6, and 7.

Chapter 3 discusses the challenges of studying social processes, such as meaning-making, emotion, and identity, through Big Data and computational methods. We describe our computational pluralist framework that combines computational methods and interpretive analysis. We also discuss the ethical considerations involved in studying white supremacists through digital data.

Chapter 4 introduces Stormfront and its users through descriptive statistics. While this chapter is not essential for the argument pursued in this book, it elaborates on the distinctive affordances of the community and explores how the technical infrastructure conditions the specific social processes that transpire within the forum.

The subsequent three chapters conduct empirical explorations of the dimensions emerging from this Durkheimian perspective to online polarization.

Chapter 5 investigates the discursive processes that occur on Stormfront that lead to the formation of a shared identity among members. Drawing on Durkheim's and Collin's works, we examine online interactions as a form of repeated rituals, in which words become markers of community belonging and barriers to outsiders. The chapter uses computational methods to examine the gradual lexical changes that signal the integration of new members into the community. Members, over time, begin viewing themselves as part of the group, absorbing its in-outgroup distinctions, and taking up jargon and emotional expressions that separate inside from outside. The shifting language captures how members develop new stories about themselves and their role in the social world. These changes are central to their identity and the foundations of their emotional lives.

In Chapter 6, the focus is on the emotional dimensions of these Durkheimian community processes. To examine these processes, the chapter looks at the impact of the 2008 election of Barack Obama on the Stormfront community. The election was a traumatic event for many white supremacists, forcing them to reconsider their established values and worldviews, upsetting the very grounds upon which their identity and self-value rested. Stormfront functioned as a form of digital therapy group, in which members collectively interpreted their emotional reactions, thereby shaping an emotionally energized collective, with a focused target of collective action.

Chapter 7 examines the discursive dimensions of these social processes and how the formation of a community leads to the construction of a shared worldview. While the stories are cultural stuff that defines the community identity – they are also representative of a particular understanding of the world that ultimately shapes action. Digital spaces are thus innovative spaces for discursive experimentation, providing fertile soil for the growth of fringe worldviews and conspiracy theories. The link between community identity and stories about the world means that communities tend to construct their own reality, in which information is evaluated based not on conformity to common standards of evidence or correspondence to a common understanding of the world but on whether it supports the community values and goals and is vouchsafed by tribal leaders. This leads to what can be called a tribal epistemology. Empirically, the chapter compares the effects of the 2008 election of Barack Obama and the 2016 election of Donald Trump on the Stormfront community, looking at how members collectively and discursively transformed these events into opportunities for the movement.

In Chapter 8, we conclude by reflecting on the broader implications of our novel insights into the impact of social media on contemporary political life. By synthesizing the empirical findings presented in the previous chapters, we delve into how the social processes occurring within online extremist communities are reshaping the current political landscape.

References

Agnew, R. (2010). A general strain theory of terrorism. *Theoretical criminology*, 14(2), 131–153.

Alexander, J. C. (2004). Toward a theory of cultural trauma. In J. C. Alexander, R. Eyerman, B. Giesen, N. Smelser, & P. Sztompka (Eds.), *Cultural trauma and collective identity*. Berkeley: University of California Press.

Bail, C. (2022). *Breaking the social media prism: How to make our platforms less polarizing.* Princeton: Princeton University Press.

Bail, C. A., Argyle, L. P., Brown, T. W., Bumpus, J. P., Chen, H., Hunzaker, M. F., ... Volfovsky, A. (2018a). Bail. *Proceedings of the national academy of sciences,* 115(37), 9216–9221.

Bail, C. A., Argyle, L. P., Brown, T. W., Bumpus, J. P., Chen, H., Hunzaker, M. F., ..., Volfovsky, A. (2018b). Exposure to opposing views on social media can increase political polarization. *Proceedings of the national academy of sciences,* 115(37), 9216–9221.

Bélanger, J. J., Nisa, C. F., Schumpe, B. M., Gurmu, T., Williams, M. J., & Putra, I. E. (2020). Do counter-narratives reduce support for ISIS? Yes, but not for their target audience. *Frontiers in psychology,* 11, 1059.

Benford, R. D. (1997). An insider's critique of the social movement framing perspective. *Sociological inquiry,* 67(4), 409–430.

Benford, R. D., & Snow, D. A. (2000). Framing processes and social movements: An overview and assessment. *Annual review of sociology,* 26(1), 611–639.

Berinsky, A. J. (2017). Rumors and health care reform: Experiments in political misinformation. *British journal of political science,* 47(2), 241–262.

Binder, J. F., & Kenyon, J. (2022). Terrorism and the internet: How dangerous is online radicalization? *Frontiers in psychology,* 13. 1–10.

Bowman-Grieve, L. (2009). Exploring "Stormfront": A virtual community of the radical right. *Studies in conflict & terrorism,* 32(11), 989–1007.

Bruner, J. (1991). The narrative construction of reality. *Critical inquiry,* 18(1), 1–21.

Butler, J. (2002). *Gender trouble.* New York: Routledge.

Caiani, M. (2018). Radical right cross-national links and international cooperation. In J. Rydgren (Ed.), *The Oxford handbook of the radical right* (pp. 394–411). London: Oxford University Press.

Caiani, M., Della Porta, D., & Wagemann, C. (2012). *Mobilizing on the extreme right: Germany, Italy, and the United States.* London: Oxford University Press.

Castaño-Pulgarín, S. A., Suárez-Betancur, N., Vega, L. M. T., & López, H. M. H. (2021). Internet, social media and online hate speech. Systematic review. *Aggression and violent behavior,* 58, 101608.

Castells, M. (2008). The new public sphere: Global civil society, communication networks, and global governance. *The annals of the American academy of political and social science,* 616(1), 78–93.

Collins, R. (2004). *Interaction ritual chains.* New Jersey: Princeton University Press.

Collins, R. (2012). C-escalation and d-escalation. *A theory of the time-dynamics of conflict. American sociological review,* 77(1), 1–20.

Della Porta, D. (1995). *Social movements, political violence, and the state: A comparative analysis of Italy and Germany.* Cambridge: Cambridge University Press.

Della Porta, D. (2018). Radicalization: A relational perspective. *Annual review of political science,* 21, 461–474.

Dubois, E., & Blank, G. (2018). The echo chamber is overstated: The moderating effect of political interest and diverse media. *Information, communication & society,* 21(5), 729–745.

Ekman, M. (2018). Anti-refugee mobilization in social media: The case of soldiers of Odin. *Social media+ society,* 4(1), 1–11.

Eyerman, R. (2004). Cultural trauma: Slavery and the formation of African American identity. In J. C. Alexander (Ed.), *Cultural trauma and collective identity* (pp. 60–111). Berkeley: University of California Press.

Eyerman, R. (2022). *The making of white American identity.* Oxford: Oxford University Press.

Farkas, J., Schou, J., & Neumayer, C. (2017). Cloaked Facebook pages: Exploring fake Islamist propaganda in social media. *New media & society,* 20(5), 1850–1867.

Ganesh, B. (2020). Weaponizing white thymos: Flows of rage in the online audiences of the alt-right. *Cultural studies,* 34(6), 892–924. https://doi.org/10.1080/09502386. 2020.1714687

Institute for Economics & Peace. (2019). Global Terrorism Index 2019: Measuring the impact of terrorism, Sydney. http://visionofhumanity.org/reports

Haller, A., & Holt, K. (2019). Paradoxical populism: How PEGIDA relates to mainstream and alternative media. *Information, communication and society,* 22(12), 1665–1680.

Hamm, M. S., & Spaaij, R. (2017). *The age of lone wolf terrorism.* Columbia University Press.

Haraway, D. (1985). A manifesto for cyborgs: Science, technology, and socialist-feminism in the 1980s. *Socialist review,* 80, 65–108.

Hassan, G., Brouillette-Alarie, S., Alava, S., Frau-Meigs, D., Lavoie, L., Fetiu, A., … Rousseau, C. (2018). Exposure to extremist online content could lead to violent radicalization: A systematic review of empirical evidence. *International journal of developmental science,* 12(1–2), 71–88.

Heft, A., Knüpfer, C., Reinhardt, S., & Mayerhöffer, E. (2021). Toward a transnational information ecology on the right? Hyperlink networking among right-wing digital news sites in Europe and the United States. *The international journal of press/politics,* 26(2), 484–504.

Jasser, G., McSwiney, J., Pertwee, E., & Zannettou, S. (2021). 'Welcome to #GabFam': Far-right virtual community on Gab. *New media & society,* 25(7), 1728–1745. https://doi.org/10.1177/14614448211024546

Jenkins, H. (2006). *Convergence culture: Where old and new media collide.* New York: New York University Press.

Jungherr, A., Rivero, G., & Gayo-Avello, D. (2020). *Retooling politics: How digital media are shaping democracy.* Cambridge: Cambridge University Press.

Karell, D., Linke, A., Holland, E., & Hendrickson, E. (2023). "Born for a storm": Hard-Right social media and civil unrest. *American sociological review,* 00031224231156190.

Karlsen, R., Steen-Johnsen, K., Wollebæk, D., & Enjolras, B. (2017). Echo chamber and trench warfare dynamics in online debates. *European journal of communication,* 0267323117695734.

Keuchenius, A., Törnberg, P., & Uitermark, J. (2021). Why it is important to consider negative ties when studying polarized debates: A signed network analysis of a Dutch cultural controversy on Twitter. *PloS one,* 16(8), e0256696.

Khader, M. (2016). *Combating violent extremism and radicalization in the digital era.* New York: IGI Global.

Koehler, D. (2014). The radical online: Individual radicalization processes and the role of the Internet. *Journal for deradicalization,* (1), 116–134.

Koster, W., & Houtman, D. (2008). Stormfront is like a second home to me: On virtual community formation by right-wing extremists. *Information, communication and society,* 11(8), 1155–1176.

Lewandowsky, S., Ecker, U. K., Seifert, C. M., Schwarz, N., & Cook, J. (2012). Misinformation and its correction: Continued influence and successful debiasing. *Psychological science in the public interest,* 13(3), 106–131.

Liang, C. S., & Cross, M. J. (2020). White crusade: How to prevent right-wing extremists from exploiting the internet. *Geneva centre for security policy*, 11, 1–27.

Marwick, A., Clancy, B., & Furl, K. (2022). Far-right online radicalization: A review of the literature. *The bulletin of technology & public life*. https://doi.org/10.21428/bfcb0bff.e9492a11

McCauley, C., & Moskalenko, S. (2008). Mechanisms of political radicalization: Pathways toward terrorism. *Terrorism and political violence*, 20(3), 415–433.

McCombs, M. E., Shaw, D. L., & Weaver, D. H. (1997). *Communication and democracy: Exploring the intellectual frontiers in agenda-setting theory*. New York: Routledge

McDonald, K. (2018). *Radicalization*. New York: John Wiley & Sons.

McKelvey, T. (2001). Father and son team on hate site. *USA Today*. Gannett Company. https://web.archive.org/web/20190124073507/https://usatoday30.usatoday.com/life/2001-07-16-kid-hate-sites.htm

McPherson, M., Smith-Lovin, L., & Cook, J. M. (2001). Birds of a feather: Homophily in social networks. *Annual review of sociology*, 27(1), 415–444.

McQuail, D. (1987). *Mass communication theory: An introduction*. New York: Sage Publications, Inc.

Melucci, A. (1996). *Challenging codes: Collective action in the information age*. Cambridge: Cambridge University Press.

Miller, C., & Graves, H. (2020). *When the 'Alt-right' hit the streets: Far-right political rallies in the Trump era*. Southern Poverty Law Center.

Miller-Idriss, C. (2022). *Hate in the homeland. In hate in the homeland*. Princeton, NJ: Princeton University Press.

Müller, K., & Schwarz, C. (2020a). Fanning the flames of hate: Social Media and hate crime. http://dx.doi.org/10.2139/ssrn.3082972

Müller, K., & Schwarz, C. (2020b). From hashtag to hate crime: Twitter and anti-minority sentiment. Available at SSRN 3149103.

Mundt, M., Ross, K., & Burnett, C. M. (2018). Scaling social movements through social media: The case of Black Lives Matter. *Social media + society*, 4(4), 205630 5118807911. http://dx.doi.org/10.1177/2056305118807911

Nyhan, B., Reifler, J., Richey, S., & Freed, G. L. (2014). Effective messages in vaccine promotion: A randomized trial. *Pediatrics*, 133(4), e835–e842.

Pariser, E. (2011). *The filter bubble: What the internet is hiding from you*. New York: Penguin Press.

Perry, B. J. (1996). A declaration of the independence of cyberspace. In J. Casimir (Ed.), *Postcards from the net: An intrepid guide to the wired world* (pp. 365–367). London: Allen and Unwin.

Perry, B., & Scrivens, R. (2016). White pride worldwide: Constructing global identities online. In J. Schweppe, & M. Walters (Eds.), *The globalisation of hate: Internationalising hate crime* (pp. 65–78). New York: Oxford University Press.

Polkinghorne, D. E. (1988). *Narrative knowing and the human sciences*. New York: Suny Press.

Ravndal, J. A. (2016). Right-wing terrorism and violence in Western Europe: Introducing the RTV dataset. *Perspectives on terrorism*, 10(3), 2–15.

Ravndal, J. A. (2018). Right-wing terrorism and militancy in the Nordic countries: A comparative case study. *Terrorism & political violence*, 30(5), 772–792.

Raymond, E. (1999). The cathedral and the bazaar. *Knowledge, technology & policy*, 12(3), 23–49.

Rodino, M. (1997). Breaking out of binaries: Reconceptualizing gender and its relationship to language in computer-mediated communication. *Journal of computer-mediated communication*, 3(3), JCMC333.

Sageman, M. (2004). *Understanding terror networks*. Philadelphia: University of Pennsylvania Press.

Sageman, M. (2008). The next generation of terror. *Foreign policy*, (165), 37. https://foreignpolicy.com/2009/10/08/the-next-generation-of-terror/

Sarbin, T. R. (1986). Narrative psychology: The storied nature of human conduct. In T. R. Sarbin (Ed.), *Narrative psychology: The storied nature of human conduct* (pp. 3–21). New York: Praeger.

Shirky, C. (2008). *Here comes everybody: The power of organizing without organizations*. New York: Penguin Press.

Simi, P., & Futrell, R. (2006). Cyberculture and the endurance of white power activism. *Journal of political & military sociology*, 34(1), 115–142.

Simi, P., & Futrell, R. (2015). *American Swastika: Inside the white power movement's hidden spaces of hate*. New York: Rowman & Littlefield.

Sunstein, C. (2002). *Republic.com*. Princeton: Princeton University Press.

Sunstein, C. (2007). *Republic.com 2.0*. Princeton: Princeton University Press.

Sunstein, C. (2008). Neither Hayek nor Habermas. *Public choice*, 134(1–2), 87–95.

Törnberg, A., & Nissen, A. (2022). Mobilizing against Islam on social media: Hyperlink networking among European far-right extra-parliamentary Facebook groups. *Information, communication & society*, 0, 1–19. https://www.tandfonline.com/doi/citedby/10.1080/1369118X.2022.2118546?scroll=top&needAccess=true

Törnberg, A., & Wahlström, M. (2018). Unveiling the radical right online: Exploring framing and identity in an online anti-immigrant discussion group. *Sociologisk forskning*, 55(2–3), 267–292.

Törnberg, P. (2022). How digital media drive affective polarization through partisan sorting. *PNAS*, 119(42), e2207159119. https://doi.org/10.1073/pnas.2207159119

Tsesis, A. (2017). Terrorist speech on social media. *Vanderbilt Law Review*, 70, 651.

Valentini, D., Lorusso, A. M., & Stephan, A. (2020). Onlife extremism: Dynamic integration of digital and physical spaces in radicalization. *Frontiers in psychology*, 11, 524.

Veilleux-Lepage, Y., & Archambault, E. (2019). Mapping transnational extremist networks an exploratory study of the soldiers of Odin's Facebook network, using integrated social network analysis. *Perspectives on terrorism*, 13(2), 21–38. https://www.jstor.org/stable/26626863

Weinberger, D. (2007). *Everything is miscellaneous: The power of the new digital disorder*. London: Macmillan.

Whittaker, J. (2022). Rethinking online radicalization. *Perspectives on terrorism*, 16(4), 27–40.

Wiktorowicz, Q. (2005). *Radical Islam rising: Muslim extremism in the West*. London: Rowman & Littlefield Publishers.

Wolfowicz, M., Hasisi, B., & Weisburd, D. (2022). What are the effects of different elements of media on radicalization outcomes? A systematic review. *Campbell systematic reviews*, 18(2), e1244.

1   Situating Stormfront in Social Media Debates

Since the Enlightenment, the possibility for people to meet and engage in public debate has been seen as a precondition of democracy. The leading figures of the Enlightenment argued for the exercise of human reason as the only legitimate foundation for the use of political power. Decisions of the era of the despotic regimes of Kings may have been based on prejudice, faith, or entrenched ideas, but in the new era, they were to be subjected to the tests of rational argument and empirical evidence. The Enlightenment gave birth to the idea of a sovereign people – a *public* – that would arrive at such well-founded positions through rational deliberation in the *public sphere*. The examples of such public spheres drew on the coffeehouses of London and Paris, in which the public gathered around the time of the French Revolution to debate the latest news.

In the centuries since, the notion of "public sphere" has been at the core of how we understand both democracy and public meeting spaces. When people are given the opportunity to come together, the outcome is inevitably debate and deliberation. The notion has, at the same time, also been subject to significant debate. As we will see, the type of online space that Stormfront epitomizes – a fringe world defined by a distinct worldview – has become central to these debates, speaking to questions not only of how to understand the societal consequences of the internet but also of the relationship between public debate and democracy. But while the high-minded theoretical debates have focused on how to understand these spaces, few attempts have been made to empirically study what, in fact, takes place within them.

In this chapter, we will situate Stormfront in the long academic debate on the relationship between the public sphere and political life to show how what takes place within this online space has implications for larger debates on media and politics. We will look at the history through which social media is seen, and we will draw on this history to argue for an alternative way to conceptualize spaces such as Stormfront. We will argue for viewing Stormfront through a social lens, focusing on the processes taking place within it and how they are affecting their participants.

DOI: 10.4324/9781003108344-2

We will argue that what takes place in digital spaces does, in fact, share much in common with the lives of the old European coffeehouses that public sphere scholars draw on as metaphors. But those historical spaces were never well-described as spaces of merely "rational deliberation". The coffeehouses were intense emotional spaces that shaped shared identities, worldviews, and values. The spaces were characterized by nuanced and complex social processes, driving the emergence not only of ideas but of the *political subject* that fought in the French and American revolutions.

We begin, however, with situating this debate in the history of the public sphere.

The History of the Habermasian Public Sphere

Jürgen Habermas (1989) was central to developing the modern notion of the "public sphere" through his famous analysis of the drivers of European Enlightenment. Habermas saw the advent of the printed press as nothing short of a bedrock for the unfolding of modern democratic life and drew on the notion of the "public sphere" to understand its transformative effects, particularly in relation to the shift from absolutist to liberal-democratic regimes.

Habermas focused in particular on the periodical press – a novelty that began to take root in Europe during the late seventeenth and eighteenth centuries – as it emerged as a vibrant platform for public debate. In the bustling towns and cities of early modern Europe, periodicals became intertwined with a variety of new social centers. Coffeehouses, in particular, came to serve as dynamic spaces where individuals could meet and debate on a level playing field. The cost of coffee was a mere penny, but the wealth of information available – through newspapers, books, magazines, and captivating conversations– came without a price. Given their intellectual richness, these coffeehouses earned the moniker of "penny universities", testifying to their role as the nerve centers of enlightening dialogue and exchange.

The new periodicals were intricately woven into the social fabric of these coffeehouses, being avidly read aloud and debated by patrons engrossed in the burning issues of the day. For Habermas, this interplay catalyzed the emergence of "the public" – constituted, in some sense, by a blend of media and physical meeting spaces. The coffeehouses furnished a political platform separate from both the state and the market, populated by private citizens congregating to address public concerns. Habermas defines the public sphere as "a realm of our social life in which such a thing as public opinion can be formed" (Habermas, 1989, p. 105). Habermas' notion depicts an arena where discussions about the "common good" can be had on a rational basis without regard for the participants' identities or status.

According to Habermas, the public sphere was crucial to render the state accountable to citizenry. When individuals met as peers in spaces allowing for open and unrestricted discourse and the bracketing of inequalities, the result was a form of coming together. The manner and medium of this confrontation were pivotal: it was the public use of reason, with private individuals engaging in dialogue. The form of rationality and mode of speech itself were shaped by the medium of the printed press, embodying the austere rationality and emphasis of long-form arguments modeled on the written discourse of printed media (see also McLuhan, 1996; Postman, 2005).

In France, coffeehouses became bastions of subversion, playing a decisive role in the 1789 upheavals. As Jules Michelet noted, "those who assembled day after day in the Café de Procope saw, with a penetrating glance, in the depths of their black drink, the illumination of the year of the revolution". In this turbulent time, "everyone spoke to each other, irrespective of distinctions (of rank): during this moment of upheaval, the rich mixed with the poor, and did not disdain to speak to them as equals" (Haine, 1998, p. 209). The cafés, and the intellectual ferment they fostered, thus laid the groundwork for the emergence of revolutionary ideologies – exemplified by Camille Desmoulins' famous call to arms from atop a café table.

Given its frequent role as a nexus for the production and dissemination of state-critical ideas, the public sphere often aroused the suspicion of the powerful. This was particularly apparent in Britain following the 1660 restoration of the monarchy. Concerned by the subversive ideas emanating from the coffeehouses, Charles II decided to suppress them. In 1675, he attempted to shut the coffeehouses down, declaring them as a "Disturbance of the Quiet and Peace of the Realm", and even tried to criminalize coffee. Yet Charles soon found his power had boundaries. People defied the King's order and continued to drink coffee. The King was forced to quietly rescind, issuing a second proclamation to nullify the first "out of princely consideration and royal compassion" (Pollan, 2022).

Failing to curb the influence of coffeehouses, authorities shifted their focus to stifling the press by imposing special taxes on newspapers and periodicals. A notable example is the British Stamp Act of 1712, which mandated newspaper proprietors to pay one penny per printed sheet and one shilling for each advertisement. The British Stamp Acts were vehemently opposed, and they became a rallying point in the struggle for press freedom. In the British colonies in America, the 1765 Stamp Act served as a catalyst for the American Revolution. The importance of an independent press during these events is evident in the inclusion of press freedom in the First Amendment to the Constitution by the American colonists, following their successful war of independence against the British Crown.

When Habermas wrote his influential book on the rise and fall of the public sphere in 1962, he nostalgically looked back on the critical rational debates that once permeated the era of the printing press. He argued that the public sphere had since deteriorated due to institutional developments tied to the advent of electrification and broadcast media such as radio and television. As public readings and debates over pamphlets and newspapers in salons and coffeehouses were supplanted by family gatherings around the television in the confines of the private home, the formerly vibrant forum of rational-critical debate was relegated to another sphere of cultural consumption. In this progression of commodification, the realm of rational-critical debate was thus replaced by consumption, allowing organized private interests to encroach upon the public sphere. Habermas asserted that the commercialization of media fundamentally transformed their character, precipitating the collapse of the public sphere into performances, image creation, and opinion management, which he perceived as typical of the television era.

A Digital Public Sphere?

The internet's early days were seen by many scholars as a potential harbinger for the revival of Habermas' critical-rational public from its long hibernation during the television era. The internet seemed to facilitate public debates, reminiscent of the discussions that took place in the coffeehouses, and was thus seen as heralding a new era of democratization (Butsch, 2011; Dahlgren, 2005). Social media eliminated the need for centralized gatekeepers or broadcasters, allowing anyone to participate in public debate. Audience participation, through posting, commenting, and "liking", seemed to promise a rebirth of the revolutionary coffeehouse dynamics, but now occurring via mediated interactions on digital platforms. Dahlgren (2005), for instance, suggested that social media serves as "communicative spaces in society that permit the circulation of information, ideas, and debates, ideally in an unfettered manner" (p. 148). The internet would, according to these scholars, enable a return of the public sphere, increasing citizens' engagement with political discussion (Holt, 2004).

It was in the context of these debates that the notion of "echo chamber" first emerged, coined by scholars who were less optimistic about the democratic consequences of digitalization. These scholars pointed out that social media would also bring about a fragmentation of the media, by diversifying offerings and enabling individuals to avoid exposure to disagreement (Gripsrud et al., 2010; Splichal, 2012). The public deliberation that took place in coffeehouses centrally hinged on *diverse* individuals coming together, allowing a consensus to be reached through rational argumentation. Social media, however, facilitates the avoidance of dissenting opinions, leading individuals to occupy divergent social spaces – and, as a result, different social realities. The internet thereby enables the public sphere to split into what Cass Sunstein (2002, 2007) calls "deliberative enclaves" or "echo chambers" – groups that are more or less insulated from one another (Bruns, 2019; Pariser, 2011). Consequently, Sunstein argued, the internet not only amplifies fragmentation but also serves as a "breeding ground for group polarization and extremism" (2002: 67). Certain opinions, ideas, or beliefs are reinforced through repetition within a closed system, creating a "reinforcing spiral" that stymies the flow of alternative or competing ideas (Slater, 2007). According to this perspective, deliberation within homogeneous groups solidifies and intensifies beliefs rather than moderating them through rational exchange, thereby pushing individuals toward more extreme political positions. Instead of converging into a rational public that counterbalances those in power, this results in a narrow perspective and extreme polarization of opinions.

While the concepts of "public sphere" and "echo chambers" represent opposite views on the effects of social media in democratic life, they, at the same time, share many common assumptions. The echo chamber stems from the same Habermasian theoretical heritage as the public sphere, viewing meetings with different perspectives as core to democratic reasoning. The two perspectives share common assumptions of politics as rooted in rational arguments around shared information and knowledge, leading to opinions and political views. As such, they both view social media in the light of rational deliberation, casting the polarizing and radicalizing power of social media predominantly in terms of opinions and issue-positions. Social media is thus mainly seen as a platform for political deliberation. The key difference between the two is that the echo chamber describes social media as fragmented and divided, while the public sphere casts it as an integrated unified space – deemed necessary for a functioning public sphere.

However, while Habermas depicted the public sphere as a unified entity, viewing its increasing fragmentation with the rise of broadcast media as a harbinger of its decay, later scholars have argued that the public sphere was always – and *should* be – fragmented and pluralistic. The influential feminist scholar Nancy Fraser (1990), for instance, suggests viewing the public sphere as consisting of a multitude of partially overlapping, partially competing spheres that may be in conflict with each other, some dominant, others subordinate (see also Warner, 2002).

Consider, for instance, Habermas' much-praised European coffeehouses. These spaces were exclusively male, leading Fraser to argue that masculinist gender constructs were inherent in the very conception of the republican public sphere that these coffeehouses embodied. However, women were welcome in the teahouses, which began appearing in 1717. Here, they could sample and purchase tea leaves to brew at home, fostering, in many ways, an equivalent vibrant culture of tea parties among upper- and middle-class women. This culture was inextricably linked with its own printed media and political debates and often positioned itself in conflict with the male public sphere – the teahouses were even at the forefront of political campaigns to shut down the coffeehouses.

To articulate these struggles among plural interacting spheres, each associated with its own print and broadcast media, Fraser (1990) introduced the notion of "subaltern counterpublics". This concept refers to parallel arenas "where members of subordinated social groups invent and circulate counter-discourses, which in turn permit them to formulate oppositional interpretations of their identities, interests, and needs" (Fraser, 1990, p. 67). Counterpublics serve specifically as sites where members of marginalized or historically disadvantaged groups can come together to contest and alter dominant public discourses (see also Felski & Felski, 1989; Ryan, 1992). The concept has historically primarily been used to conceptualize how "good" or "progressive" groups formulate alternative identities, interests, and needs internally through in-group discussions and then promote these counter discourses externally to a wider public. Nevertheless, the notion of counterpublics has more lately been broadened and has increasingly been applied to examine also non-marginalized conservative or reactionary groups that perceive their opinions to be suppressed (see e.g. Holm, 2019; Kaiser, 2017; Toepfl & Piwoni, 2015, 2018; Törnberg & Wahlström, 2018).

The diverse spaces come with their own forms of rationality and discourse. Fraser criticized Habermas for lacking a power perspective and advocating a specific type of masculine rationality as something universal (Fraser, 1990). Craig Calhoun similarly criticizes Habermas for the naïve notion that "identities and interests [are] settled within the private world and then brought fully formed into the public sphere" (Calhoun, 1992, p. 35). In this sense, Habermas is argued to have treated publics predominantly as spheres for rational-critical discourse, presupposing participants who can engage in argumentation, make judgments based on reasons, and be free of social and economic pressures.

The emphasis on debate and discursive contestation has also meant a lack of attention to other important aspects of social and political life taking place within these spaces. By positioning the publics primarily as arenas of discursive contestation, the Habermasian approach has been criticized for overlooking the roles of emotion, embodiment, partiality, passion, and subjectivity within the public sphere (e.g. Johnson, 1998; Mouffe, 1999; Sanders, 1997). This bias toward rational discourse tends to dismiss the potential emotional roles publics can fulfill for their participants and how it may foster a community of reasoners. This relates to significant questions about social identity and agency. Other scholars have nuanced this critique, arguing that it relies on the false assumption that emotions are radically distinct from rationality and emotion is in no way incompatible within Habermas' framework (Gutmann & Thompson, 2009; Krause, 2011; Neblo, 2007). Regardless, the critique rightly points out that Habermas did not as thoroughly explore the implications of his theory of emotions with the same systematic rigor applied to other key concepts, leaving the connection between deliberative theories and empirical studies of emotion in deliberation underdeveloped. This neglect of emotional processes and the formation and enactment of social identities is prevalent in much of the academic tradition on social media that builds on his work. For instance, Neblo (2020) notes that the term "emotion" is notably absent from a recent review article on experiments in democratic deliberation (Gastil, 2018).

Although Fraser (1990) arguably expands the notion of subaltern counterpublics somewhat by focusing on their roles as arenas for the "formation and enactment of social identity", her focus still lies on counterpublics as issue-specific discursive arenas that help to "expand discursive space" and contribute to "widening of discursive contestation" (p. 67). The agency incorporated in these concepts of the public primarily concerns a form of agency that can be captured by rather passive verbs like judge, scrutinize, and decide. As Warner (2021) has argued, more active, externally oriented verbs can only be attributed to the agency of other collective entities like crowds or social movements. A public may have opinions, but a collective that acts politically must be defined as something else.

Using a distinction in social movement theory, conceptualized by Klandermans (1984), one might say the typical activities associated with publics and counterpublics pertain to *consensus mobilization* – that is, creating support for certain perspectives on an issue. However, the literature on publics seldom relates directly to what Klandermans terms *action mobilization* – that is, motivating those who agree on an issue to take joint action to address their grievances.

To incorporate and address these aspects of online communities that relate to notions such as agency and identity, we can turn to the social movement literature. This field has undertaken a largely parallel examination of counterpublics, using terms such as *free spaces* (Evans, 1979), *social movement communities* (Buechler, 1990), *safe spaces* (Gamson, 1996), *cultural laboratories* (Taylor, Whittier & Morris, 1992), *submerged networks* (Melucci, 1989, 1996), *abeyance structures* (Taylor, 1989), and more recently, *dense sub-cultural networks* (Diani, 2013). As Polletta (1999, p. 1) eloquently notes, these terms typically encapsulate the "small-scale settings within a community or movement that are removed from the direct control of dominant groups, are voluntarily participated in, and generate the cultural challenge that precedes or accompanies political mobilization". This body of literature hence offers a fundamentally different perspective on the nature of free spaces, diverging from the critical-rational conception of the public. Instead, the processes unfolding within these spaces are depicted as emotional and subjective, resulting in a shared identity, energy, and action – in short, producing political subjects.

Free spaces are considered crucial for political mobilization (see e.g. Asen, 2000; Polletta, 1999; Warner, 2002). On the one hand, they fulfill *inward-oriented* objectives for movements, serving as sanctuaries for retreat and regroupment. They provide refuge from the dominant society and hegemonic ideologies, constituting a shielded space where new radical ideas, social practices, collective identities, and collective-action frames can emerge, thereby shaping our perceptions of both existing and new problems, their causes, and consequences. In this sense, they offer an opportunity for those who experience exclusion or marginalization to come together and cultivate a sense of collectivity, which is crucial for acting as a collective. On the other hand, they also provide space for *outward-oriented* objectives, aiding the dissemination of radical ideas and promoting collective action by facilitating the development of strategies, information sharing, evaluation of tactics, improvement of public speaking skills, creation of campaigns, leadership training, and recruitment of new activists (Simi & Futrell, 2009, 2015).

The notion of free spaces has traditionally been used to depict relatively small-scale settings in the physical world. A classic example of this can be found in the black churches in the American South, which can be traced back to the abolishment of slavery at the end of the 18th century (Calhoun-Brown, 2000). These churches provided a sanctuary where black people could congregate, a haven offering temporary respite from the horrors of slavery and, later, from Jim Crow segregation. They served as focal points for black communities and facilitated aid and comfort for escaped slaves, all away from the gaze of white society. These spaces were crucial in forging a collective identity and a shared sense of resistance. In a similar vein, the Mosques and Bazaars of the Arab were crucial venues for challenging dominant public discourse, but they fostered relationships and social networks that encouraged collective action (Bennani-Chraïbi & Fillieule, 2003; Hessler, 2011).

Free spaces are intrinsically linked to social movements, often functioning as incubators for movement organization by providing essential social, cultural, and emotional resources. These spaces provide a sanctuary where like-minded individuals can gather to express their views, forge identities, devise, strategize, and mobilize without fear of external control, reprisal, or societal marginalization. However, free spaces serve a broader purpose beyond merely providing a venue for movements; they are often instrumental in sculpting the trajectories of movement cycles. Scholars have long emphasized the interplay between movements and their (physical) spaces, suggesting that spaces are active participants that shape the movements which they incubate, imprinting their cultures and their forms of sociality.

The Civil Rights movement, for instance, was shaped and defined by its origins in black churches; the prayers, rituals, music, and doctrines of the church became part of the movement and, importantly, anchored it in the doctrine of the equality of men before God. The Christian context engendered in its members an oppositional consciousness and sacrificial resistance that predisposed them to challenging society while maintaining that acts of protest must be carried out within the bounds of the law. This provided the context for the evolution of a strategy of non-violent social action, which resonated with the oppositional civil culture that the church cultivated: challenging systematic injustices and racism while embracing the principles of liberal society. Non-violence was preached as the way through which early Christians fought injustices and was said to still be a guide for good Christians to fight injustices anywhere in the world. In this way, the religious setting contributed to the philosophy of non-violent resistance that came to dominate the civil rights movement.

Similarly, the Parisian working-class cafes shaped the French Revolution of 1848. The informal and spontaneous egalitarianism that took place around the coffee tables inspired and forged the spirit of the French revolution. In some cases, even the physical setting of the cafeterias was central for the revolutionary movement, serving as protective shelters during the violent riots with the police, and tables, chairs, carafes, and crockery turned into projectiles. Even some more aesthetic aspects of the revolution can be traced back to the cafeterias: the bawdy and ribald vocabulary around the cafeterias came to characterize the revolutionary propaganda, and the first "bonet rouge" – the distinctive headgear of the movement – was donned in the café *Procope*. In both these cases, social interaction was typically limited to relatively small-scale settings, often limited to friends and family.

Digitalization of Politics

As we have seen, the dominating debate on the effects of the digitalization of politics has been between "public spheres" or "echo chambers". Whereas the former suggests that digitalization has brought a reinvigoration of the public sphere, the other side claims that it has brought fragmentation and division. Both sides of the argument, however, share much of the same Habermasian understanding of what constitutes a healthy public sphere: a single egalitarian arena of critical-rational deliberation around shared facts.

However, the literature on counterpublics and free spaces challenge these assumptions by offering a profoundly different view on the nature of a functioning plural democracy. They propose that it is something more akin to a mosaic or a web of partially overlapping and partially conflicting publics. The political life that takes place within these spaces goes far beyond mere rational deliberation, arguments, and opinions; they shape identities, communities, and ways of reasoning about the world.

What does this imply for the central debate with which we began: what is the impact of digitalization on the political life of this complex web of publics? What takes place within these digital spaces, and how do they affect the lives of their participants?

In examining the effects of digitalization, we must consider its associated fragmentation, individualization, and globalization as not merely amplifying extreme opinions by distorting rational deliberation. Instead, they are reshaping processes in the realm of collective identity, emotions, and discourse. Just as the black churches shaped the movements that they incubated, the architectures of the digital environment – algorithms, designs, and code – are active mediators, becoming intertwined with and altering the social dynamics of political life.

The social understanding of digital spaces calls for a corresponding framework for understanding the basic building blocks of political life. As this book seeks to examine what takes place within the digital spaces that incubate the extremist movements of the day, we need to first develop a theory to guide our empirical study. In the following chapter, we will develop such a framework, drawing upon the theories of Émile Durkheim and Randall Collins.

References

Asen, R. (2000). Seeking the "counter" in counterpublics. *Communication theory,* 10(4), 424–446.

Bennani-Chraïbi, M., & Fillieule, O. (2003). Résistances et protestations dans les sociétés musulmanes [Resistances and protests in Muslim societies. The press of the National Foundation of Political Science]. *Presses de Sciences Po Paris.* https://www.cairn.info/resistances-et-protestations-dans-les-societes-mus-2724608909.htm

Bruns, A. (2019). *Are filter bubbles real?*: Hoboken, NJ: Polity Press.

Buechler, S. M. (1990). *Women's movements in the United States: Woman suffrage, equal rights, and beyond.* New Brunswick: Rutgers University Press.

Butsch, R. (2011). Audiences and publics, media and public spheres. In V. Nightingale (Ed.), *The handbook of media audiences* (pp. 147–168). Malden: Wiley-Blackwell.

Calhoun, C. (1992). Introduction. In C. J. Calhoun (Ed.), *Habermas and the public sphere.* Cambridge: MIT Press.

Calhoun-Brown, A. (2000). Upon this rock: The black church, nonviolence, and the civil rights movement. *PS: Political science and politics,* 33(2), 169–174.

Dahlgren, P. (2005). The internet, public spheres, and political communication: Dispersion and deliberation. *Political communication,* 22(2), 147–162.

Diani, M. (2013). Organizational fields and social movement dynamics. In J. Stekelenburg, C. Roggeband, & B. Klandermans (Eds.), *The future of social movement research: Dynamics, mechanisms, and processes* (pp. 145–168). Minneapolis: University of Minnesota Press.

Evans, S. M. (1979). *Personal politics: The roots of women's liberation in the civil rights movement and the new left* (Vol. 228). London: Vintage.

Felski, R., & Felski, J. (1989). *Beyond feminist aesthetics: Feminist literature and social change.* Cambridge: Harvard University Press.

Fraser, N. (1990). Rethinking the public sphere: A contribution to the critique of actually existing democracy. *Social text,* (25/26), 56–80.

Gamson, W. A. (1996). Safe spaces and social movements. *Perspectives on social problems,* 8, 27–38.

Gastil, J. (2018). The lessons and limitations of experiments in democratic deliberation. *Annual review of law and social science,* 14, 271–291.

Gripsrud, J., Moe, H., Molander, A., & Murdock, G. (2010). *The idea of the public sphere: A reader.* Lanham, MD: Lexington Books.

Gutmann, A., & Thompson, D. F. (2009). *Democracy and disagreement.* Cambridge: Harvard University Press.

Habermas, J. (1989). *The structural transformation of the public sphere: An inquiry into a category of bourgeois society.* Cambridge: Polity.

Haine, W. S. (1998). *The world of the Paris café: Sociability among the French working class, 1789-1914.* Baltimore: Johns Hopkins University Press.

Hessler, P. (2011). The Mosque in the Square. *The New Yorker.*

Holm, M. (2019). *The rise of online counterpublics?: The limits of inclusion in a digital age.* Uppsala: Department of Government, Uppsala University. https://uu.diva-portal.org/smash/record.jsf?pid=diva2%3A1329534&dswid=-1939

Holt, R. (2004). *Dialogue on the internet: Language, civic identity, and computer-mediated communication.* Westport: Blomsbury Publishing.

Johnson, J. (1998). Arguing for deliberation: Some skeptical considerations. In J. Elster (Ed.), *Deliberative democracy* (pp. 161–184). Cambridge: Cambridge University Press.

Kaiser, J. (2017). Public spheres of skepticism: Climate skeptics' online comments in the German networked public sphere. *International journal of communication*, 11, 1661–1682.

Klandermans, B. (1984). Mobilization and participation: Social-psychological expansions of resource mobilization theory. *American sociological review*, 49(5), 583–600.

Krause, S. R. (2011). Empathy, democratic politics, and the impartial juror. *Law, culture and the humanities*, 7(1), 81–100.

McLuhan, M. (1996). *Understanding media: The extensions of man.* Barcelona: Las Marinas.

Melucci, A. (1989). *Nomads of the present: Social movements and individual needs in contemporary society.* New York: Vintage.

Melucci, A. (1996). *Challenging codes: Collective action in the information age.* Cambridge: Cambridge University Press.

Mouffe, C. (1999). Deliberative democracy or agonistic pluralism? *Social research*, 66(3), 745–758.

Neblo, M. A. (2007). Family disputes: Diversity in defining and measuring deliberation. *Swiss political science review*, 13(4), 527–557.

Neblo, M. A. (2020). Impassioned democracy: The roles of emotion in deliberative theory. *American Political science review*, 114(3), 923–927.

Pariser, E. (2011). *The filter bubble: What the Internet is hiding from you.* UK: Penguin.

Pollan, M. (2022). *This is your mind on plants.* New York: Penguin Press.

Polletta, F. (1999). "Free spaces" in collective action. *Theory and society*, 28(1), 1–38.

Postman, N. (2005). *Amusing ourselves to death: Public discourse in the age of show business.* New York: Penguin Books.

Ryan, M. P. (1992). Gender and public access: Women's politics in nineteenth-century America. In C. Calhoun (Ed.), *Habermas and the public sphere* (pp. 259). Cambridge: MIT Press.

Sanders, L. M. (1997). Against deliberation. *Political theory*, 25(3), 347–376.

Simi, P., & Futrell, R. (2009). Negotiating white power activist stigma. *Social problems*, 56(1), 89–110.

Simi, P., & Futrell, R. (2015). *American Swastika: Inside the white power movement's hidden spaces of hate.* Lanham: Rowman & Littlefield.

Slater, M. D. (2007). Reinforcing spirals: The mutual influence of media selectivity and media effects and their impact on individual behavior and social identity. *Communication theory*, 17(3), 281–303.

Splichal, S. (2012). *Transnationalization of the public sphere and the fate of the public.* New York: Hampton Press.

Sunstein, C. (2002). *Republic. Com.* Princeton: Princeton University Press.

Sunstein, C. (2007). *Republic.com 2.0.* Princeton: Princeton University Press.

Taylor, V. (1989). Social movement continuity: The women's movement in abeyance. *American sociological review*, 54(5), 761–775.

Taylor, V., Whittier, N., & Morris, A. (1992). Collective identity in social movement communities: Lesbian feminist mobilization. In A. Morris, & C. Mueller (Eds.),

Frontiers in social movement theory (pp. 104–129). New Haven: Yale University Press.

Toepfl, F., & Piwoni, E. (2015). Public spheres in interaction: Comment sections of news websites as counterpublic spaces. *Journal of communication*, 65(3), 465–488.

Toepfl, F., & Piwoni, E. (2018). Targeting dominant publics: How counterpublic commenters align their efforts with mainstream news. *New media & society*, 20(5), 2011–2027.

Törnberg, A., & Wahlström, M. (2018). Unveiling the radical right online: Exploring framing and identity in an online anti-immigrant discussion group. *Sociologisk forskning*, 55(2–3), 267–292.

Warner, M. (2002). Publics and counterpublics. *Public culture*, 14(1), 49–90.

Warner, M. (2021). *Publics and counterpublics*. New York: Zone Books.

2   A More Social Theory of Online Politics

As we have seen, existing research has started from the assumption that politics within social spaces fundamentally hinges on *deliberation*: the articulation of rational arguments for or against a particular position. This perspective has fostered the concept of radicalization as a gradual accumulation of one-sided arguments, culminating in increasingly extreme opinions.

In this chapter, we offer another understanding of the activity unfolding within these spaces. Drawing on Durkheim's and Collins' work on community formation, we aim to develop and apply a theory of the social processes transpiring within digital spaces. We suggest that what takes place in these spaces has less to do with deliberation and has more in common with the dynamics of a *ritual*.

The exploration of rituals by Durkheim and Collins provides an intricate framework for discerning the nature of social interaction and its social implications. Rather than cold rationality, the notion of rituals emphasizes that common activity constitutes the social glue of a community. This theory postulates that as individuals gather around a common interest, this interest tends to transform into a collective identity, simultaneously articulated in a discourse that serves to demark insiders from outsiders and functions as linguistic capital within the community. We argue that online communities like Stormfront weave from political exchange into a form of digital tribe – with a shared sense of collective self, a distinct worldview, and a potent emotional drive to engage in collective action.

To expand our theoretical framework for understanding how individuals are affected by their participation in online political discussions, we must journey back to the turn of the 20th century, to the dancing flames of a campfire in rural Australia.

Durkheim and the Social Function of Campfires

Beneath the star-studded skies of the outback, a group of Aboriginals are gathered, their faces bathed in the warm glow of the flames. The gentle rustling of leaves and the subtle hum of distant wildlife punctuate the air as stories

DOI: 10.4324/9781003108344-3

unfurl – tales of their ancestors, the latest gossip, or their hunting bravados – all unfolding to the choreography of the fires leaping embers. In this shared moment, they find comfort and connection, a profound sense of belonging that binds them together as a community. This seemingly niche setting was the subject of study for one of the principal founders of modern sociology: Émile Durkheim.

Through anthropological studies of these Aboriginal communities, Durkheim sought to decipher the social glue that binds communities and societies. He found that a majority of the community's time was consumed by everyday activities involving only a subset of the group, such as gathering food or tending to children. The rare events in which the entire tribe would gather for shared rituals were seen as sacred. Within these rituals, the tribe would engage in synchronized movements and chanting which brought the tribe to trance-like states – a phenomenon Durkheim referred to as *collective effervescence*. These states imbued the participants with emotional energy and a sense of intersubjectivity. The focus of the community's attention was on common objects, resulting in a shared emotion that integrated the group as a whole. This is what made the community a *community* rather than just a collection of individuals.

The objects at the heart of these rituals became imbued with the community's emotional energy and intersubjectivity, thereby evolving into sacred objects for the community. In the tribes, Durkheim studied, the totem served as the central object of common attention. Its presence during these gatherings transformed it into a physical representation of the group's experience and a symbol of the emotional energy generated throughout the collective rituals. The totem became a communal emblem, channeling and perpetuating the energy from the community's rituals into their everyday life. Symbols and shared experiences thus form the building blocks of an internal culture, mirroring the community's interconnectedness.

Scholars have since expanded and reinterpreted Durkheim's findings to provide insights into contemporary society. Collins (2004), in particular, incorporated ideas from Erving Goffman to recontextualize Durkheim's work into a micro-sociological theory on how groups cultivate social membership and intersubjectivity – essentially, their collective identity as a *"we"*. Collins, like Durkheim, places rituals at the center – those moments of shared attention and emotion. He perceived these moments as capable of transforming objects of shared attention into symbols charged with group belonging. These symbols subsequently play a part in further rituals, fostering a chain of interaction that constitutes the foundation for the shared sense of community. Collins invokes the concept of rituals in a broad sense: dancing together at a club, collectively chanting at a Trump rally, or even the simple act of sharing a cigarette.

According to Collins, such rituals play a crucial part in generating collective emotions and building a sense of shared identity among individuals. Collins argues that rituals create a mutual focus of attention among participants.

By engaging in specific actions, words, and symbolic gestures, individuals synchronize their behavior, which leads to a heightened emotional energy within the group. These chains of interactions are characterized by mutual attentiveness, emotional entrainment, and a sense of solidarity. The shared emotions experienced during rituals create a powerful sense of belonging and a collective identity that transcends individual differences. This emotional energy is contagious and spreads throughout the community, fostering a collective effervescence. Symbolic objects, gestures, and rituals carry shared meanings that bind individuals together and create a common understanding. These symbols serve as a framework through which individuals interpret and make sense of their social world, reinforcing social bonds and group cohesion. According to Collins, rituals also have a micro-level effect on individuals' emotional state. Through the repeated practice of rituals, individuals acquire emotional skills and learn to manage their own emotions. This emotional management contributes to a sense of emotional trust and predictability within the community, enhancing social bonds and cooperation.

While the notion of ritual is focused on the physical spaces, we will here seek to adapt it to understand the online world.

Bringing Durkheim Online

While both Durkheim and Collins viewed physical co-presence as a necessary precondition for successful rituals, recent work suggests that these rituals can also occur in mediated environments (DiMaggio et al., 2018; Johannessen, 2023; Maloney, 2013; Wästerfors, Burcar Alm, & Hannerz, 2023). Although online interaction rituals may be lower in intensity, this is compensated by their often sustained and long-term nature. A similar argument is made by McCaffree and Shults (2022), who argue that social cohesion in modern societies is maintained through "distributive effervescence", consisting of less intense but more frequent encounters. Along these lines, Campos-Castillo and Hitlin (2013) have emphasized the relevance of *perceived* copresence and treat bodily copresence as one variable among several that contribute to this perception. Studies have also suggested several other factors that enable entrainment in lieu of bodily copresence, including that social media may facilitate finding and meeting other hard-to-reach individuals with similar interests and shared knowledge – factors that tend to facilitate the mutual focus of attention and shared mood (Cetina, 2009; DiMaggio et al., 2018; Rettie, 2009).

The digitalization of interaction rituals also shifts the emphasis from the physical to the discursive. As non-physical meetings limit the possibilities for physical artifacts serving as barriers for entry or markers by which one may build confidence that the person with whom one is conversing is indeed an insider (Maloney, 2013), the interaction rituals and their effects instead take place in the realm of words and stories (Benwell, 2006) – suggesting the need of adapting Collins' framework (cf. Colombo & Senatore, 2005).

In its offline formulation, Collins (2004) posits that interaction rituals have four key components: *group assembly, barriers to outsiders, mutual focus of attention,* and a *shared mood.* These components partly overlap and feed into one another, with the mutual focus of attention and common mood reinforcing each other, for example. The presence of these components results in four outcomes: *group solidarity, common standards of morality, sacred objects,* and *emotional energy in individuals.* The ingredients and the outcomes form a feedback loop: a chain of interaction that serves as the foundation of communities.

This view can be applied to social media, as shown in Figure 2.1. In this context, the interaction ritual takes the form of the exchange of messages on a shared topic. In other words, the rituals are conversations. From the point of view of social membership, conversations are significant not so much for their content, but rather as a moment of shared focus on a common activity: like any ritual, they can be constituted by a shared focus on a shared set of symbols combined with a shared emotion. The difference, of course, is that the four ingredients and the four outcomes are fulfilled by the realm of ideas, discourse, and language. The objects of the shared attention are words, stories, and images, rather than a physical object, and it is these words, stories, and images that convey the shared experience.

The sense of *group assembly* is provided by the common banner under which individuals have gathered. While digital spaces cannot provide a sense of shared physical space, they do feature designs and descriptions that demark the purpose and shared focus of the community: the logo, name, description,

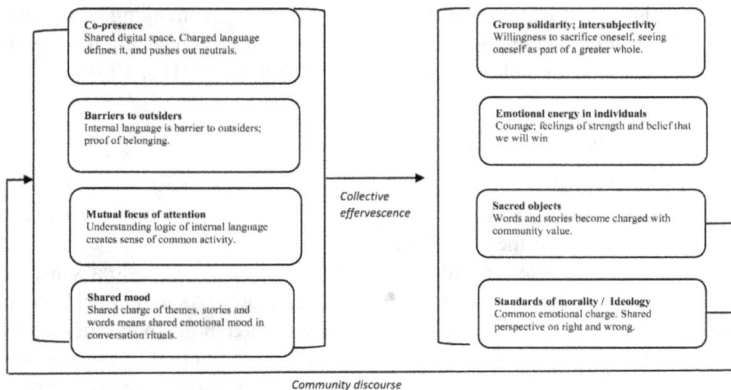

Co-presence	Group solidarity; intersubjectivity
Shared digital space. Charged language defines it, and pushes out neutrals.	Willingness to sacrifice oneself, seeing oneself as part of a greater whole.
Barriers to outsiders	**Emotional energy in individuals**
Internal language is barrier to outsiders; proof of belonging.	Courage; feelings of strength and belief that we will win.
Mutual focus of attention	**Sacred objects**
Understanding logic of internal language creates sense of common activity.	Words and stories become charged with community value.
Shared mood	**Standards of morality / Ideology**
Shared charge of themes, stories and words means shared emotional mood in conversation rituals.	Common emotional charge. Shared perspective on right and wrong.

Collective effervescence

Community discourse

Figure 2.1 This figure adapts Collins' (2004) illustration, which summarizes his theoretical framework. It is modified here to describe online communities, demonstrating how discourse and language symbols fulfill the symbolic functions that Collins outlines.

and graphic designs provide the foundation on which a common cognitive reality is gradually constructed. Digital spaces are so designed to raise a banner declaring the shared attributes around which the community gathers.

As part of this, the community over time develops certain *barriers to outsiders*, taking the form of an internal culture and language. These are ways of determining who is part of a community, and who is not. Some such markers can be technically encoded in the digital space, for instance, through information such as a number of user posts or community status, or the possibility to choose a recognizable username or picture. The most important means of determining insiders from outsiders, however, lies in the discursive realm; certain words, themes, stories, ideas, or images come to serve as emblems and evidence of group membership. (This will be discussed in more detail below.)

As communities meet around shared interests, these give rise to certain shared topics and themes that comprise the *mutual focus of attention*. Certain topics become typical for the community, and the conversations will tend to center around these topics. Online meeting places are furthermore technologically structured so as to allow the conversations to share topics – forums, for instance, have subforums and discussion threads, which organize the conversations to make sure participants have a mutual focus of attention.

The stories, languages, and local knowledge that become characteristic of a community not only function as membership emblems and cultural capital for the community but also carry a certain emotional charge, creating the experience or feeling of a *shared mood*. As members learn the discourse of the community, they also learn what to feel about different topics and stories. The specialized language of the community has a symbolic value and is charged with a special excitement, tension, or enthusiasm through conversation rituals. This is part of what makes them powerful tools for invoking a common cognitive reality in conversation rituals, functioning as conversational or cultural resources that invoke "a shared reality" (Collins, 1981, p. 1001).

Effects of Successful Digital Rituals

The effects of rituals can be categorized into two classes: first, *intersubjectivity*, *collective identity*, and *emotional energy*; second, a community *discourse* that contains within it the community and its ideology.

First, a central effect of successful rituals is that they create a sense of *group solidarity*, strengthening their collective identity. As individual participants develop a stronger sense of solidarity and intersubjectivity, they come to also assume the thoughts, morals, and behaviors internal to their group, viewing themselves less as individuals and more as part of the community. The ritual, in short, transforms a group of individuals into a community; a shared sense of "we".

Participants experience rituals as a pleasant experience, filling them with what Collins calls *emotional energy*: a positive feeling that makes participants want to stay in the community, often manifested as confidence, warmth, and enthusiasm. This is, in other words, the dopamine boost that many media scholars have described as being a central driver of social media use and which can even lead to addiction. This emotional energy is what drives members to act on behalf of the community in other settings, such as participating in a demonstration – or perhaps storming the US Capitol.

Second, the rituals are based on the elaboration of a discursive system: the objects of shared attention are the topics, concepts, beliefs, and interests around which the community is gathered. Some of these can come to function as symbols of the community. Durkheim found that objects that were the center of attention of rituals became filled with emotional energy and came to represent the community. These objects become sacred as the community "reifies its experience, makes it thing-like, and thus an emblem, treated as having noun-like permanence" (Collins, 2004, p. 37). For the tribes that Durkheim studied, the main object of common attention was the totem, but Collins broadened the concept considerably. For online communities, the object of shared attention is the topics, concepts, beliefs, terms, and interests around which the community is gathered, which thus become symbols of the community. Just like the sacred objects in the physical rituals described by Collins and Durkheim, these symbols are used as part of further rituals, becoming the cultural items that create a chain of interaction rituals that constitutes the foundation of the shared sense of community. These cultural items are charged up with membership significance through repeated ritualistic interactions, making these symbols not only indicative of the group but the very stuff through which intersubjectivity is constructed and maintained.

These discursive symbols come to form the linguistic capital through which rituals are enacted, both as emblems of group membership and as indicative of a shared moral foundation (Collins, 2004). The internal language provides barriers to outsiders, ensuring that only those who are "in the know" can participate. This function can be seen in how meme culture tends to exhibit complex layers of intertextual references, abstract and ironic styles, constantly in flux and innovation, requiring both literacy and dedication to decode and stay up to date with the latest trends (Knobel & Lankshear, 2007; Shifman, 2013). This challenge is precisely the point (Phillips & Milner, 2017), as this language functions to create a subcultural definition of cultural capital in opposition to the mainstream culture. These subcultures thus define forms of distinction through a linguistic market, conferring cultural capital and authority on those who master the language (Bourdieu, 1991). This separates outsiders from insiders through the demarcation of those who are unaware of the subcultural logic and values of the community.

However, the community discourse is not merely an arbitrary collection of language games. The community's discourse expresses a political subjectivity and embodies the community ideology: what is seen as good and what is evil (Durkheim, [1912] 1915). The formation of a collective identity is necessarily also the creation of difference; as Benhabib (1996, p. 3) puts it, "every search for identity includes differentiating oneself from what one is not" – identifying the in-group with good and casting as evil what lies outside the group's boundaries. Since the identification of shared similarities neces-sarily implies the creation of a difference – a sense of what the community values and what it opposes – this discursive system comes to define *common standards of morality.* For Durkheim, identity was formed through opposition to the devil and a striving for similarity with a God, ascribed through the ritu-als of regular participation in religious services. In applying this to the broader context of group formation, the bond of similarity can be made in opposition to an outside force – which, in turn, becomes the personification of evil. This conflictual element of group solidarity can be more or less dominant for dif-ferent groups but is a central driver of violence, extremism, and intergroup conflict. In this sense, the interaction ritual is a micro-sociological mecha-nism for generating both the "glue" that holds social groups together and the "energy" to initiate social change and dominate others.

From the ingredients and effects of these social rituals, we can identify three intertwined dimensions in which online communities act: they create a shared sense of *identity* by elaborating a shared *worldview*, filling them with *emotional* energy. These three dimensions of community life will guide our further exploration, as they provide the foundation for political subjects that are driven and energized to engage in political action.

Identity: Spaces for Collective Identification

A community's reasoning about the world leads to its formation as a creat-ing subject. As it creates its view of the world, it also creates a view of itself: a collective identity. Digital communities hence transform shared interests into collective identities and a sense of community. Digital spaces serve as arenas where individuals see themselves in others, leading to a common un-derstanding of "we" or seeing the "we" in "me" (Cohen, 1985; Melucci, 1989; Touraine, 1985). This common understanding is considered the basis and pre-requisite for collective action in the social movement literature.

Worldview: Spaces for Interpreting Reality

In the Durkheimian perspective, being part of a community involves sharing a worldview. Language and the social are mutually constitutive, with lan-guage constructing social and political reality while also being influenced by it. Language is thus seen as an ideological practice that mediates, influences, and even constructs our experiences, identities, and perspectives on the world. Digital communities provide spaces for movements to produce their own sto-ries about the world. Unlike the printed press, that established a foundation of shared facts that then became subjects of debate in coffeehouses, social media has limited separation between facts and their debates. Movements originating from fringe digital spaces often seem to come with their own unique understanding of the world – their own version of reality based on complex conspiracy theories that are disconnected from reality and society at large.

Digital spaces do give space to the elaboration of worldviews – but not through the critical-rational process described by Habermas. The reasoning about the world is inextricably interlinked with the formation of a community – its goals, its aims, and its hopes. As the community grows in importance, it defines its own framework for making sense of the world – what we may term a "tribal epistemology". The implication is that events in the world are interpreted not through rational reasoning on the basis of known facts but rather by what story can be told that best fits the values and aspirations of the tribe. As community identity grows in importance, we thereby become susceptible to conspiracy theories and misinformation – losing our ability to distinguish between what is supported by evidence and what we wish were true.

Emotions: Spaces for Verbalizing and Transforming Emotions

The stories we tell about the world are simultaneously stories about ourselves and our role in the world. Such stories are more than just told; they are viscerally *felt*. They link us to our social world and the communities from which we draw safety. While Habermas treated the reasoning as merely rational, we suggest that political life is centrally emotional. The processes of articulation and verbalization involved in making sense of the world at the same time transform emotions, processing traumas, and turning passive emotions into the emotional energy that drives political action.

We have now proposed a theoretical perspective on how interaction in digital spaces results in the development of group identity and internal culture. In essence, our argument is that echo chambers do not result in the divergence of opinions, but rather they shape communities with a shared sense of self, unique worldviews, and a heightened emotional energy to participate in collective action. This is how social media is transforming political life. These three dimensions will serve as the framework for the book's empirical examinations in Chapters 5–7.

References

Benhabib, S. (1996). *Democracy and difference: Contesting the boundaries of the political*. Princeton: Princeton University Press.

Benwell, B. (2006). *Discourse and identity*. Edinburgh: Edinburgh University Press.

Bourdieu, P. (1991). *Language and symbolic power*. Cambridge: Harvard University Press.

Campos-Castillo, C., & Hitlin, S. (2013). Copresence: Revisiting a building block for social interaction theories. *Sociological theory*, 31(2), 168–192.

Cetina, K. K. (2009). The synthetic situation: Interactionism for a global world. *Symbolic interaction*, 32(1), 61–87.

Cohen, J. (1985). Strategy or identity: New theoretical paradigms and contemporary social movements. *Social research*, 52(4), 663–716.

Collins, R. (1981). On the microfoundations of macrosociology. *American Journal of sociology*, 86(5), 984–1014.

Collins, R. (2004). *Interaction ritual chains*. New Jersey: Princeton University Press.

Colombo, M., & Senatore, A. (2005). The discursive construction of community identity. *Journal of community & applied social psychology*, 15(1), 48–62.

DiMaggio, P., Bernier, C., Heckscher, C., & Mimno, D. (2018). Interaction ritual threads: Does IRC theory apply online? In E. B. Weininger, A. Lareau, & O. Lizardo (Eds.), *Ritual, emotion, violence* (pp. 99–142). New York: Routledge.

Durkheim, E. ([1912] 1915). *The elementary forms of the religious life*. New York: Free Press.

Johannessen, L. E. (2023). Interaction rituals and technology: A review essay. *Poetics*, 98, 101765.

Knobel, M., & Lankshear, C. (2007). Online memes, affinities, and cultural production. *A new literacies sampler*, 29, 199–227.

Maloney, P. (2013). Online networks and emotional energy: How pro-anorexic websites use interaction ritual chains to (re) form identity. *Information, communication & society*, 16(1), 105–124.

McCaffree, K., & Shults, F. L. (2022). Distributive effervescence: Emotional energy and social cohesion in secularizing societies. *Theory and society*, 51, 1–36.

Melucci, A. (1989). *Nomads of the present: Social movements and individual needs in contemporary society*. New York: Vintage.

Phillips, W., & Milner, R. M. (2017). Decoding memes: Barthes' punctum, feminist standpoint theory, and the political significance of# yesallwomen. In S. Harrington (Ed.), *Entertainment values: How do we assess entertainment and why does it matter?* (pp. 195–211). London: Palgrave.

Rettie, R. (2009). Mobile Phone communication: Extending Goffman to mediated interaction. *Sociology*, 43(3), 421–438.

Shifman, L. (2013). Memes in a digital world: Reconciling with a conceptual troublemaker. *Journal of computer-mediated communication*, 18(3), 362–377.

Touraine, A. (1985). An introduction to the study of social movements. *Social research*, 52(4), 749–787.

Wästerfors, D., Burcar Alm, V., & Hannerz, E. (2023). The bumpy paths of online sleuthing: Exploring the interactional accomplishment of familiarity, evidence, and authority in online crime discussions. *New media & society*, 0(0), 14614448221149909. https://doi.org/10.1177/14614448221149909

3 Methodology, Data, and Ethics

Paradigms often come with research methods. As the prevailing debate between public spheres and echo chambers has assumed that heterogeneous interaction fosters moderation and homogeneous interaction incites radicalization, the current research paradigm has tended to emphasize the *structure* of social interaction. As a result, social network analysis has been used to provide a quantitative view into the patterns of interaction, allowing conclusions to be drawn about the possible polarizing consequences of a particular platform.

However, if we relinquish the assumption that interaction necessarily implies rational deliberation, these dominant methods become inadequate. It then becomes necessary to carry out a more profound examination of the content and meaning of interactions and how participation in these spaces is affecting the meaning-making, emotion, and identity of participants. This calls for a fundamentally different methodological toolkit compared to those that have predominantly dominated the field thus far. In this chapter, we will therefore delineate our approach to studying the Stormfront community.

Digital Ethnography

Digitalization has not only brought about a shift in the lives of social movements, but the data generated by digital platforms has also afforded researchers a new lens through which to study these lives. Access to detailed longitudinal data has unveiled new opportunities for tracing individuals and their actions, as well as for analyzing large-scale discursive shifts.

Social movement scholars have predominantly focused on the overt and public activities of social movements, such as demonstrations, speeches, and public manifestos, despite the fact that these external activities represent only a small fraction of social movement activities. Digital data grants researchers access to the "backstage" of social movements, unveiling what Alberto Melucci (1989) has referred to as "latent movement activities" – the "invisible" networks of everyday life. As we have saw in the previous discussion on free spaces and counterpublics, these spaces, or "cultural laboratories", are often

DOI: 10.4324/9781003108344-4

where the initial steps towards counteracting the sense of powerlessness are taken. They play a crucial role in assisting individuals to reclaim a sense of agency rather than remaining passive victims or bystanders, whether the movement actors are progressive and reaching out to discriminated, marginal, or subaltern groups or conservative activists who perceive their opinions as being repressed. These activities are thus politically significant, as they help cultivate actors who view themselves as capable of political action, which is often a prerequisite for other forms of activism.

While accessing this type of data has historically been a difficult task, often confined to time-consuming ethnographic studies, the advent of social media and digital platforms such as Facebook, Twitter, and various internet forums in recent decades has opened up unique possibilities for empirical inquiry. Internet communities like Stormfront provide an opportunity to observe the latent phases of movements: the inner workings and processes where alternative values, discourses, and practices are generated, negotiated, and enacted. This inside view allows researchers to see the details of the political life of individuals, the bottom-up collective processes through which they construct a worldview that simultaneously serves as the foundation for a sense of common identity.

However, this also raises challenging ethical, methodological, and epistemological questions. The questions asked in this book concern issues such as emotions, storytelling, meaning-making, and identity – aspects of human life that have historically been firmly located in the realm of interpretive and qualitative research. The study of meaning-making requires interpretation – Weber's *Verstehen* – which is associated with qualitative methods.

But with a dataset of over 10 million posts involving over 350,000 individuals spanning over 20 years, traditional qualitative methods, such as close-reading, are not a viable path. It would take years just to read through the material, and, more fundamentally, it would make it impossible to trace the subtle shifts in discourse and language of individual users over the years that signify their descent into extremism.

Traditionally, the aims of this project would have been almost a non-starter. Sociologists have had to choose between either the intensive and in-depth qualitative methods or the extensive but from a distance view of quantitative methods. However, the nature of digital data and methods means that this is no longer necessarily the case. The Stormfront dataset is an example of digital data that can be studied using powerful new methods that cut across the traditional quantitative-qualitative divide. This raises the potential for answering qualitative questions in large data materials – that is, to *interpret* Big Data.

For the examination of Stormfront, in particular, the core tenet here is the combination of interpretation and computational methods. The approach can, therefore, be described as a form of "digital ethnography" or "netnography" (Kozinets, 2010; Lindgren, 2017). Digital ethnography is based on ethnographic principles but blends computational methods of data collection, analysis, coding, and visualization with more traditional qualitative and interpretative analysis. As the sociologist Simon Lindgren (2017, p. 274) suggests, employing social media as a research instrument offers "a new kind of microscope, which we can use to shed light on both new issues that are specific to digital society, and on basic and longstanding questions about human social life".

The primary aim of ethnographic research is to provide "thick descriptions" of the patterns and functions of social life, which are characterized by details, conceptual structures, and meaning, as opposed to "thin" descriptions that merely provide facts without interpreting them. The method for achieving such thick descriptions varies depending on the material under study. While traditional ethnographic methods have often relied on interviews, long-term observations, and engagement in the field, the definition of "field" is changing in the digital age, and computational methods can now be considered new forms of ethnographic methods. To gain a rich and detailed understanding of the milieu being studied, we thus need to expand the classic toolbox of ethnography. As Kozinets (2015, p. 79) suggests, the study of sociality online must be about "intelligent adaptation" and "considering all options" while maintaining the core principles of ethnography. It should seek to systematically seize "the possibilities of incorporating and blending computational methods and data collection, analysis, word recognition, coding, and visualization".

In this way, computational methods are thus integrated into the interpretative tradition of ethnography. The versatility and multidimensionality of digital data require a multilayered research process that alternates between quantitative and qualitative methods. In this sense, a "methodological promiscuity" may be necessary to combine techniques and develop strategies that are as appropriate as possible to the research question asked.

Digital ethnography, or netnography, has several advantages over traditional ethnographic approaches. First, traditional approaches have been criticized for providing merely "ethnographic snapshots" – that is, data limited to a certain time span, to a relatively small number of activists, and a limited part of the environment. In contrast, digital data typically provide longitudinal and detailed data enabling, for example, to study the interplay between individual members and emerging social structures and norms within online communities, as well as how specific historical events have affected the movement.

Second, traditional ethnographic data collection is often time-consuming and requires building trust and strong interpersonal relationships with members of the movement, which may even be dangerous in the case of extreme right groups that actively intimidate researchers (Blee, 1998). Online ethnography allows for a "distanced insider" perspective, providing a unique insight into hidden "latent" social conditions and enabling a systematic and method-based empirical analysis of movement internal processes. Like traditional ethnographic research, online ethnography can capture "intersubjective, complex, highly fluid, rapidly shifting phenomena [...] which are missed by macro level analysis" (Juris, 2008, p. 38)

Digital research also presents certain peculiarities, in which it requires a contextual understanding of digital data. Digital data is unique in the sense that it is not produced for scientific consumption but rather a by-product consisting of traces of our digital lives. However, this does not imply that digital data is neutral or objective. As Kitchin (2014, p. 5) has stated, "[Big] Data are not simply natural and essential elements that are abstracted from the world in neutral and objective ways and can be accepted at face value; data are created within a complex assemblage that actively shapes its constitution". Digital data is not a mere "trace" of social reality, but rather a constructed representation that reveals some aspects while concealing others. In the case of Stormfront, the community has a certain architecture that shapes the interaction on the forum. Moderators and administrators have the power to move and delete posts as they see fit. Individual users are given a "reputation" based on a rating system, which may shape how much influence they have in the discussions. Paying users may obtain a higher status than non-paying members and have access to private sections of the forum. The division of the forum into certain sub-forums also shapes what discussions are favored (These features are discussed in more detail in Chapter 4). In this sense, digital data is inevitably imbued with power and shaped according to certain interests, which we need to be aware of when conducting digital research. While this may not necessarily need to be at the forefront of any actual analysis based on digital data, an awareness of this should certainly characterize the research process. Therefore, digital ethnography needs to be *critical* (Törnberg & Uitermark, 2021)

Digital ethnography provides an important philosophical ground on which to stand on in our examination of the Stormfront data. Next, we will describe more in practice what such a critical methodological pluralist approach may look like and how we can integrate interpretative and computational methods.

Interpreting Big Data

The computational methods employed in this book originate from various methodological families and include social network analysis, natural language processing, statistical analysis, and qualitative content analysis. These methods often scramble traditional academic research traditions by mixing and matching from quantitative and qualitative dichotomies, such as inductive *vs* deductive, internal *vs* external validity, exploratory *vs* confirmative, and so on (Törnberg & Törnberg, 2019).

We aim to leverage this blending of epistemic attributes toward what Danermark, Ekstrom, and Jakobsen (2001) call "critical methodological pluralism". This involves going beyond methodological dichotomies by combining methods and harnessing the respective strengths of interpretative social analysis and computational methods within the same framework. The challenge is to integrate interpretive and computational methods rather than, as is often the case, leaving interpretation as an afterthought to formal, automatic analyses. The goal is not to "replace" or "automate" interpretation but to incorporate it into a larger methodology that enables its application to large data materials through the inclusion of algorithmic elements (see also Nelson, 2020). This requires a multilayered research process that alternates between quantitative and qualitative methods and analyses, thereby incorporating bringing human interpretation into the process.

We will formulate a process that provides the methodological framework for the empirical analyses in this book, adapted for the specific research questions and material. This pluralist approach combines the strengths of particular methods: using automated inductive methods for mapping and exploring the corpus; qualitative methods for in-depth and interpretive analysis, statistical methods for verifying the external validity of identified pattern, and so on.

Based on an abductive approach to data analysis, this process begins with exploring the data material to identify surprising or unanticipated observations based on existing theory and knowledge. Similar to grounded theory, this approach allows the concepts to emerge from the data rather than being imposed by the researcher. It also allows for the inclusion of "subjective" aspects of the social world. These observations are then used to formulate hypotheses for further examination and testing. Finally, these hypotheses are then deductively tested. This form of causal inference is both explorative and deductive, data-driven, and theory-based.

Following this, our interpretive computational methodology consists of three analytical steps, as illustrated in Figure 3.1.

Step 1: Pattern-detection Using Computational Exploratory Analysis

The first step involves applying exploratory and inductive methods to map and provide an overview of the data, with the aim of identifying unexpected patterns based on existing theory and expectations. This exploration typically involves unsupervised pattern-finding, text mining, and clustering methods, such as topic modeling and word embedding, sentiment analysis, community detection (within social network analysis), and basic data analysis methods, such as k-means clustering or principal component analysis.

These methods can aid the exploration of large and complex datasets by reducing them into more manageable and interpretable formats and representations. By enabling comparisons and structuring, these representations suggest relevant patterns that can lead to the formulation of hypotheses. These techniques can further help researchers identify new ideas or concepts emerging from the data.

To provide a simple example, this step may consist of producing a social network based on friendship connections and using community detection to find clusters within this network. This may lead to the identification of clear divisions within the community that call for further exploration.

Figure 3.1 This figure illustrates the methodological framework taken in this book, what is here referred to as an interpretative computational methodology. This framework consists of three analytical steps that combine automated inductive analysis for exploring large amounts of texts with qualitative methods for in-depth analysis.

Step 2: Hypothesis Refinement through In-Depth Examination

In the second step, the researcher focuses on the identified patterns to interpret and analyze the data in-depth. To move from distance to close-reading, researcher can often use the maps created in the first step, which can help them select representative or characteristic texts and provide a closer examination of relevant patterns. This allows researchers to formulate and refine hypotheses for further exploration. Using computational methods in this way enables close-reading to be employed efficiently on large-scale data while making the method more systematic and rigorous by providing a framework that prevents cherry-picking or unintended introduction of researcher biases.

Continuing with the example of the friendship network, researchers can draw from each of the identified clusters a selection of the most central members for closer inspection. Looking at the posts and profiles of these members may lead to the hypothesis that the division in the communities is primarily driven by geography, with clusters representing different countries and regions.

Step 3: Testing and Confirmation through Deductive Statistical Analysis

In the first two steps, the researcher identifies unexpected patterns in their data using inductive methods, producing and refining hypotheses. In the third step, the researcher can further test and refine these hypotheses in the full corpus using more deductive methods to add further reliability and external validity. This can involve using statistics or supervised machine learning methods that operationalize a hypothesis and test whether the given pattern holds throughout the corpus.

Returning to the example, researchers can test the hypothesis that the clusters are geographically defined by quantitatively looking at the most common answer to the question "where are you from?" in the members' profile pages. Differences in these answers may reveal that this is indeed what characterizes many of the clusters. However, some of the clusters may not be characterized by any particular geographical region. To understand this, the researcher can return to step 2, focusing on these clusters, to further explore what may characterize these clusters and drive their separation from other communities.

While the term *step* is used here, it may imply a static process. However, this research process is dynamic and recursive, and shifting between different methods highlights different aspect of the phenomena. This is not traditional triangulation, which aims to validate findings through different methods. Rather, the aim is to bring different dimensions of social reality into view while constructing rigorous and reproducible approach. The methods are combined in a way that simultaneously reveals different aspects of the phenomenon, while also combining the epistemological properties of the methods. By moving between different tools and perspectives while being aware of their limitations and biases, one can construct a whole that is reliable and reproducible – thus seeing a whole world by catching various "glimpses of reality" (Byrne, 1998). While this describes the broader methodological approach taken in this book, the specific chapters will outline the particular method they employ.

Extracting Stormfront Data

The Stormfront data was collected using custom-written web scrapers, which were parallelized and ran through multiple proxies to avoid tracing. Scraping required employing various techniques to by-pass the forum's security service, particularly CloudFlare – an external security layer that aims to prevent automatic software from accessing their website. We will not describe in detail how this was done, as we do not wish to assist Stormfront in improving its digital security. The scrapers mimicked a regular user who logged into the forum, accessing threads in random order and recording page-by-page posts to a database. The scraping carried out various forms of checks to ensure that no threads were lost and handled any problems, such as missing threads, connection errors, or timeouts. This was implemented as a Python application running against a PostgreSQL database. The member page of each user on the forum was scraped in a similar way, collecting their user information, such as presentation, occupation, ideology, date of birth, friendship connections, and so on.

The data material consists of 10,172,069 posts and 354,574 members, of which 99,988 had written one or more posts. The forum was downloaded in September 2020. The data analysis was carried out using Python and standard data analysis packages such as pandas and nltk.

Ethics in Digital Research

Digital research is still in the process of establishing clear ethical standards. What is considered ethically defensible often varies dramatically between disciplines and geographical regions. Conducting research using digital data sources can entail significant risks and uncertainties and can give rise to delicate and unruly ethical dilemmas. Digital data can originate from unconventional sources, such as hacked data that have been made public, or from custom-made crawlers that may violate the rules of the community from which the data is collected (which is often the case when using data from Facebook and Instagram).

Conducting social media research thus means navigating new and messy definitions of the private and the public. This forces the researcher, among other things, to rethink traditional concepts of *informed consent, confidentiality*, and *anonymity*. New data types and collection methods raise novel ethical issues, and old ones may manifest in new ways. This means that there are no universal ethical norms or principles that can be applied across all studies. Rather than ethics as a "one-off" tick box exercise, digital research often requires a *process-driven* approach, in which ethical guidelines need to be developed on a case-by-case basis tailored for the specific research project. Researchers must engage in a reflexive process, continually reflecting on their practices and risks and engaging in dialogue with other researcher in the field.

Informed consent is a central ethical issue in research involving human participants. While it is straightforward in surveys and interviews, it can be challenging in studies involving hundreds of thousands of anonymous members on a website. Some scholars have addressed this issue by continuously posting online announcements of their presence, offering members the opportunity to withdraw from the study. However, this may not be feasible in studies involving a large public internet forum, and may impact forum dynamics, which comes with its own ethical issues.

This book follows the ethical guidelines on internet research provided by the British Sociological Association (British Sociological Association, 2017) and The Association of Internet Researchers (franzke et al., 2020). The praxis in the field of digital research is to distinguish between private and public arenas. This is based on how accessible the space is to the public, to what extent the members are aware that it is a public domain, and whether membership registration is required. Posts made in open profiles or groups addressing an unknown public are typically regarded as acceptable for academic studies without explicit author consent. In the case of Stormfront, the community is open for reading without registration, and participants are aware (and constantly remind each other) they are being monitored by authorities, journalists, and political antagonists. This is also explicitly stated in an email that each new member receives when registering on the forum. Therefore, we follow the praxis in the field and consider Stormfront as a public domain and do not require informed consent from the participants.

When data are used without explicit consent from the participants, the need for ensuring anonymity in the research is further accentuated. This is particularly relevant when collecting sensitive personal data that may involve political opinions and religious beliefs. In such cases, there may also be legal factors to consider. Protecting research participants is crucial both in the phase of collecting and storing data, as well as in the phase of publishing the results.

The collected data were stored in a safe environment. During the early phase of data collection, usernames were automatically replaced with randomized numbers to prevent the tracing of individual members. When publishing the results, all personal information and other identifiable characteristics, such as usernames and places or other people, were excluded. The focus of the analysis was generally on the broader discursive patterns. When direct quotes were used, they were slightly altered to make them harder to trace back to specific members.

We can thus conclude that conducting social research in the age of datafication demands continuous critical reflections. Rather than ethics being a box-ticking activity, we need an interdisciplinary, open, and generative approach to research ethics (Pink & Lanzeni, 2018). Another set of challenging ethical questions that we encountered when working with this book relates to our very object of study, namely right-wing extremists.

Ethics of Studying Unethical Movements

Principles and ethical guidelines in research are often specifically designed with particular actors and movements in mind. A common ethical principle is that researchers must always consider possible side-effects of their research and ensure that the participants' interests are protected by not using the material for a purpose that conflicts with their beliefs. Similarly, research must not contribute to further marginalization or stigmatization of the group under study (cf. Elgesem, 2015; Markham, 2020).

In fields such as anthropology, social movement research, activist research, and in general, all research that employs ethnographic methods, it is common to emphasize the moral virtue of collaboration, reciprocity, and advocacy. The spirit of anthropological fieldwork ethics means not only protecting informants but actively supporting their political struggles by practicing "fieldwork solidarity" and promoting the welfare of our informants and their communities. Thus, the researcher should not only be a passive observer, but the output produced should also feed back into the movement and provide a concrete contribution. This reasoning comes from the fact that most movements and actors studied tend to be progressive and environmental movements with which the researcher often sympathizes. However, what if supporting the struggles of informants is in itself unethical? What if the groups we study are not the oppressed but oppressors and the bigoted? How should these well-intended, ethical principles be interpreted when our research participants include white supremacists and neo-Nazis, whose goal is to eliminate a large proportion of the population, including Jews and political opponents? Showing solidarity with those we study may make us accomplices in acts of symbolic or real violence. In these cases, we find ourselves in a contradictory and uncomfortable position between protecting our research participants or serving a broader good.

This ethical ambiguity led the American Anthropological Association (AAA) to revise its statement on ethics in 2012. It now reads: "Anthropologists must weigh competing ethical obligations to research participants, students, professional colleagues, employers and funders, among others while recognizing that obligations to research participants are usually primary". In this revision, they replaced the original statement "Must come first" to "Usually primary". This change reveals how anthropologists have attempted to reconcile these two potentially conflicting commitments. One commitment, codified in past AAA statements and prevailing institutional review procedures, is to show solidarity with the people they study, and the other, energized by critical anthropology, is to counteract exploitation and injustice at large.

One radical solution that some ethnographers, such as Benjamin Titelbaum, in his ethnographic studies on the far-right in the Nordic countries, have embraced is advocating for an "immoral anthropology" (Teitelbaum, 2019). Titelbaum defends scholar-informant solidary as morally volatile and epistemologically indispensable. In his ethnographic studies, he went beyond the "do not harm" principle and even cultivated close and long-term relationships, which were fed by honesty, reciprocity, and trust. He even helped with far-right text production by reading and commenting on a manuscript and publicly defended one of his nationalist friends against what he perceived as unjust criticism. According to Titelbaum, friendship is a precondition for accurate, truthful understanding. It can lead to privileged insight and enable the receipt of invaluable insider evaluation.

However, many other scholars take the opposite standpoint. Kathleen Blee, in her extensive ethnographic studies on racist activities in the United States, points to the mismatch between feminist-inflicted ethical ideals and the realities of doing research with people who may be oppressive and bigoted. She notes that feminist principles require researchers to share their research with participants, "thereby leveling the inherent inequality between researcher and subject" (Blee, 1993, p. 605). Blee suggests that not only is this principle "based on romantic assumptions", but it is also doubtful that it "serve[s] any purpose" (p. 606) in the context of studying her subjects, in this case, the Ku Klux Klan. At the very least, principles such as these "assume a measure of ideological compatibility between scholar and those being studied" (Blee, 2017), which does not necessarily exist. Historian Alessandro Portelli (1997) takes a similar standpoint to what he refers to as "hostile ethnography". He argues:

> while we are bound to report as faithfully as we can what our interviewees actually said, our responsibility toward them does not extend to always agreeing with them. Sometimes our ethics as citizens, as individuals involved in the struggle for democracy, equality, freedom, and difference, may transcend the limited ethics of our profession in favour of a broader, human, and ultimately political ethics. [...] Sometimes, when we interview the rich, the mighty, the generals, it may be highly ethical to act as spies in the enemy camp.
>
> (1997, 66)

When doing digital ethnography, we avoid some of these difficult dilemmas. The researcher does not have to actively engage in the field but can remain a "distanced insider", reaping the benefits of unique insights into what is happening inside the movement but without having to acknowledge our presence. Therefore, there are no practical or instrumental reasons to build reciprocal social relationships or create trust with our informants. Likewise, we may avoid ethically dubious acts such as conscious deception or actively lying to the participants by pursuing a more subtle form of "honest dissimulation".

Nonetheless, some difficult ethical issues persist. We still face the delicate balance between protecting our informants and contributing to a more just world. Even if we accept the standpoint of feminist and critical theories, how far should we go to impede the reactionary and oppressive movements that we study? In digital research, these issues are not only thought-provoking dilemmas but also a practical reality. For instance, when scraping a website, the researcher must decide how fast and aggressively the crawlers should work: should data be collected through multiple parallel crawlers, and how long should the wait time be between each request? Intensive collection means a faster process, but it also implies higher pressure on the servers, resulting in higher costs for the owners and for small sites, potentially making the website becoming temporarily inaccessible to other users.

In this book, we have decided to chart a middle course between these contrasting ethical positions. We have chosen not to directly engage or interfere with the activities taking place on the forum but to remain distant observers. As part of this approach, we have committed ourselves to reporting any unlawful content, such as death threats or explicit calls for violence, to the relevant authorities. However, this type of material is exceedingly rare on Stormfront due to the rigorous enforcement of behavioral guidelines by the moderators. As researchers, we believe that our primary means of combatting extremism and hate is through critical analysis, public education, and fostering discussions on how to address the root causes of these movements. This book represents our contribution toward achieving these goals.

References

American Anthropological Association (AAA). (2012). Principles of professional responsibility. https://ethics.americananthro.org/category/statement/

Blee, K. (1998). Managing emotion in the study of right-wing extremism. *Qualitative sociology*, 21(4), 381–399.

Blee, K. M. (1993). Evidence, empathy, and ethics: Lessons from oral histories of the Klan. *The journal of American history*, 80(2), 596–606.

Blee, K. M. (2017). *Understanding racist activism: Theory, methods, and research*. London: Routledge.

British Sociological Association (BSA). (2017). *Ethics guidelines and collated resources for digital research*. https://www.britsoc.co.uk/media/24309/bsa_statement_of_ethical_practice_annexe.pdf

Byrne, D. S. (1998). *Complexity theory and the social sciences: An introduction*. London: Routledge.

Danermark, B., Ekstrom, M., & Jakobsen, L. (2001). *Explaining society: An introduction to critical realism in the social sciences*. London: Routledge.

Elgesem, D. (2015). Consent and information–ethical considerations when conducting research on social media. In H. Fossheim & H. Ingierd, *Internet Research Ethics* (pp. 14–34). Cappelen Damm Akademisk. https://press.nordicopenaccess.no/index.php/noasp/catalog/book/3

franzke, as, Bechmann, A., Zimmer, M., & Charles, E. (2020). *Internet Research: Ethical Guidelines 3.0*. https://aoir.org/reports/ethics3.pdf

Juris, J. (2008). *Networking futures: The movements against corporate globalization*. Durham: Duke University Press.

Kitchin, R. (2014). Big data, new epistemologies and paradigm shifts. *Big data & society*, *1*(1). https://journals.sagepub.com/doi/epub/10.1177/2053951714528481

Kozinets, R. (2015). *Netnography: Redefined, London and thousand oaks*. London: Sage.

Kozinets, R. V. (2010). *Netnography: Doing ethnographic research online*: London: Sage Publication.

Lindgren, S. (2017). *Digital media and society*. London: Sage.

Markham, T. (2020). *Digital life*. Cambridge: Polity Press.

Melucci, A. (1989). *Nomads of the present: Social movements and individual needs in contemporary society*. Philadelphia: Temple University Press.

Nelson, L. (2020). Computational grounded theory: A methodological framework. *Sociological methods & research*, *49*(1), 3–42.

Pink, S., & Lanzeni, D. (2018). Future anthropology ethics and datafication: Temporality and responsibility in research. *Social Media+ society*, 4(2), 2056305118768298.

Portelli, A. (1997). *The battle of Valle Giulia. Oral History and the art of dialogue*. Madison: University of Wisconsin Press.

Teitelbaum, B. R. (2019). Collaborating with the radical right: Scholar-informant solidarity and the case for an immoral anthropology. *Current anthropology*, 60(3), 414–435.

Törnberg, P., & Törnberg, A. (2019). Minding the gap between culture and connectivity: Laying the foundations for a relational mixed methods social network analysis. In *Mixed methods social network analysis* (pp. 58–71). London: Routledge.

Törnberg, P., & Uitermark, J. (2021). For a heterodox computational social science. *Big data & society*, 8(2), 20539517211047725.

4 Introducing Stormfront

This chapter introduces Stormfront and provides a discussion on the particular affordances of the community. In this way, it explores how the technical infrastructure conditions the specific social processes that transpire within the forum.

In many ways, Stormfront is much like any other online meeting place. Discussions are held, articles are shared, events are announced, and news are posted. While building on old technology, the forum has gradually experimented with new social functionalities, such as emojis, celebrating members' birthdays with small symbols, and essay contests with 2000 USD awards. Through these innovations, a community has emerged, forming a bubble of members with similar beliefs and interests. Stormfront runs on standard Vbulletin software, but it has a custom design and messages that serve as a flag, signaling the common ground around which the community gathers – declaring *this is who we are as a community.*

The community for which Stormfront provides a home is centered around white supremacy, anti-Semitism, conspiracy theories, and holocaust denial. Although it was initially most popular among supporters of the KKK and various neo-Nazi groups, it is by no means limited to those groups. "Any Caucasian who can talk/type and contribute to criticizing the demise of our Germanic world is welcome and even desired here", one member writes. The forum thus strives to maintain a relatively nonsectarian stance, encouraging people from different parts of the far right[1] to join.

Despite the diverse range of members, the majority of Stormfront's members are united in their adherence to a white supremacist ideology, which is symbolized on the site by a prominent logotype featuring a Celtic cross, a symbol that was used by Norwegian Nazis during World War II to symbolize white supremacy. It also looks like a rifle visor. Just in case this imagery is too subtle, the logotype is complemented by the slogans "White Pride World Wide" and "Every Month Is White History Month". The forum's stated mission is to "provide information that is not available in the controlled media and to build a community of white activists who promote the survival of our kind of people".

DOI: 10.4324/9781003108344-5

White supremacy is broadly characterized by hate-directed beliefs, feelings, and behavior toward non-whites, homosexuals, and other perceived "outgroups". White supremacy can be described as a "master status" (Hughes, 1945) that cuts across a person's multiple identities and occupies a central positive in one's daily life (Simi & Futrell, 2009). In this sense, it is a totalizing set of experiences that permeates all aspects of a person's thoughts, emotions, and actions. On Stormfront, Jews, and blacks are particularly targeted and consistently identified as outgroups, followed by Muslims, Immigrants, Latinos, and the LGBT community. These patterns remain relatively stable over time despite some fluctuations, as illustrated in Figure 4.1.

This rallying flag of white Supremacy has given rise to a violent extremist community. Stormfront has earned the moniker "the murder capital of the Internet", with Stormfront members having committed nearly 100 murders since 2010, according to the Southern Poverty Law Centre (Beirich, 2014). This trend began to accelerate in early 2009 after Barack Obama became the first black president of the United States. The most prominent example of this violence is the far-right terrorist Anders Behring Breivik, who was responsible for the 2011 terror attacks in Oslo and Utøya, which claimed the lives of 77 people, mostly young people. At the time of the attacks, Breivik had been a registered member of Stormfront for almost three years. Under the username "year 2183", Breivik introduced himself in October 2008. In one of his posts, he wrote, "Feminism, corrupt treacherous politicians, a corrupt treacherous media, pro-immigration Jewry and a corrupt academia is the hole in the 'dike,' while Muslims are the water flooding in". He was warmly welcomed by other members of the forum: "glad to have you here". Just hours before his terror attacks, Breivik sent his manifesto to two other influential Stormfront members.

Despite facing competition from new extremist online platforms, including discussions forums such as 8kun (formerly 8chan), 4chan, Voat, The Daily Stormer, Parler, and Gab, Stormfront remains one of the most important and long-lived platforms for white supremacists worldwide. Although many other extremists' sites have been taken offline by authorities or providers after some time, Stormfront has managed to remain online despite several attempts over the years and decades. As a result, the website contains more than 20 years of far-right discussions dating back to the early days of the internet.

Stormfront has been the focus of much research attention since its inception, with studies focusing on virtual community formation (Bowman-Grieve, 2009; De Koster & Houtman, 2008), collective identity (Bliuc et al., 2019; Perry & Scrivens, 2016; Simi & Futrell, 2015), recruitment processes (Lennings et al., 2010; Wong, Frank, & Allsup, 2015), cultural support for far-right activists (Caren, Jowers, & Gaby, 2012), its connection to other extremist websites (Burris, Smith, & Strahm, 2000).

Due to its longevity, the forum provides a valuable resource for analyzing the dynamics of user engagement. For example, Scrivens, Davies, and Frank (2020) examined how posting activity on Stormfront is influenced by

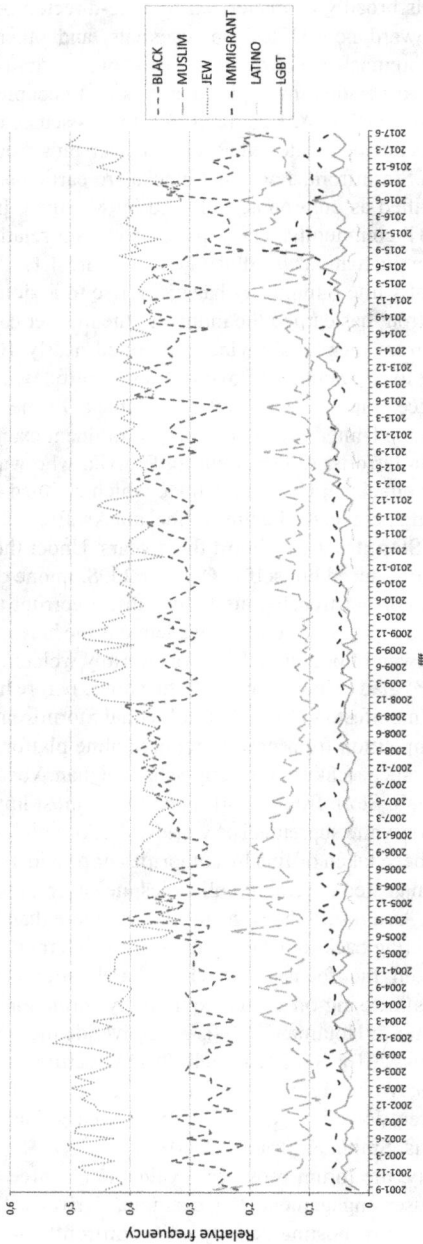

Figure 4.1 This figure illustrated distinguished outgroups on Stormfront over time. It shows that Jews and Blacks remain the primary outgroups throughout the period, followed by Muslims. The figure was constructed by calculating the relative frequency of words relating to each outgroup over time.

external political events, while Kleinberg, van der Vegt, and Gill (2021) examined trends in user activity and extremist language. Additionally, Davies et al. (2022) studied the differences in posting activity between violent and nonviolent right-wing extremists. Scholars have also investigated the broader context of online platforms, describing the existence of a far-right online ecosystem in which individual users encounter conspiracies and extremist ideas on mainstream media platforms and gaming platforms and are then gradually channeled into more radical content. This trend has been further reinforced during the COVID-19 pandemic, with several reports from authorities and security agencies suggesting that the pandemic has served as a catalyst, triggering a wave of disinformation and conspiracy theories as a result of the internet has become the primary connection to the external world for many people (SÄPO, 2021; U.S. Department of Justice, 2022).

The Demography of Stormfront

Based on self-reported statistics, Stormfront has around 350,000 members. In recent years, Stormfront has experienced a decline in the number of posts per year as well as in active membership. Despite this, it remains a significant platform for white supremacists worldwide. The community provides a venue for blogs and a daily radio show hosted by the founder, Don Black.

While the forum allows visitors to browse without registration, posting requires a sign-in. The forum is carefully administered with explicit guidelines on appropriate behavior to maintain a professional atmosphere, including refraining from personal attacks, profanity, and racial slurs and using proper spelling and grammar. Posting under only one username is also mandated. Nazi symbols and racial slurs were prevalent until their ban in the spring of 2008. Stormfront's site model follows the tactics of David Duke, who once urged his Klan followers to "get out of the cow pasture and into hotel meeting rooms". As Black stated in an interview, "We don't use the 'n——, n——' type of approaches". Regular reminders inform users that the forum is public, stating, "Don't post anything you wouldn't want attributed to you in a court of law, quoted on the front page of the New York Times, or read by your mother".

The forum has moderators and administrators who oversee specific forums, edit and delete posts, and move threads, among other responsibilities. Moderator positions are typically offered to knowledgeable and helpful users in the subject matter of the forum they moderate. Administrators exercise overall control of the community, deciding how the board is styled, which forums to create and how to organize them, what information to require from members, and who to appoint as moderators.

The forum is structured into multiple sections, including News, General Discussions, FAQ, Activism, and White Singles. Each of these sections contains sub-forums. For instance, Activism consists of Events, Strategy and Tactics, eActivism, and Multimedia, etc. The forum also includes sixteen sub-forums designed for international members, such as Europe, South Africa, Britain, Downunder, and Russia, among others. These sub-forums are predominantly utilized by individuals who speak different languages. A language detection analysis confirms that English is the most commonly used language, accounting for 88.6% of all posts, followed by Dutch (2.8%), Italian (1.8%), and Spanish (1.3%). Additionally, the forum has an open section for guests and political opponents interested in white nationalism.

In 2008, Stormfront created a private "sustaining members" section exclusively for those who provide financial support to the forum. This section has become a sanctuary for the most influential members of the community. Sustaining members have access to additional features, such as a larger mailbox and four times bigger avatars. However, we refrained from accessing this section to avoid financially supporting the community.

Members can send private messengers to each other, establish "friendships", and form "social groups" consisting of individuals with shared interests. This provides a way of communicating between members as well as sharing photos or other images. Social groups can be both public and require an invitation. Another common feature is "reputation", which is a way of rating users depending on the quality of their posts. If a member has written many posts that have received a high reputation, the member obtains a high reputation score. The forum also allows you to rate threads between 1 star (terrible) and 5 stars (excellent). This appears next to the thread names and affects how many readers it gets.

Regarding site traffic, most visitors are from the United States (around 50%), primarily the Western and Southern regions.[2] However, many members also hail from countries such as the United Kingdom, Canada, the Netherlands, and Australia. Direct traffic (60%) and Google searches account for most of the site's traffic, while other extremist sites, such as Metapedia.org, Theapricity.com, and Dailystormer, as well as Wikipedia, are the top-referring sites, according to Alexa. Audience overlap analysis indicates that typical Stormfront visitors also frequent other extremist sites like Theapricity.com, Metapedia, Rightpedia, Vnnforum, Jewornotjew.com, Voat.co, and 8ch.net, along with the Southern Poverty Law Center, suggesting a significant proportion of the visitors may be ideological opponents.

Compared to many other social media platforms, the average member of Stormfront is relatively old. This may be due in part to the fact that the community is attracting fewer new members, as younger individuals tend to gravitate toward mainstream online platforms such as YouTube or Discord or alt-right platforms like Gab, Seen.life, Voat, Dailystormer, and 8chan.

Upon registration, members have the option to describe their occupation. The pie chart presented in Figure 4.2 displays the distribution of occupation categories among Stormfront members as self-reported and categorized according to the International Standard Classification of Occupations (ISCO) structure. It should be noted that this estimate is approximate, as open text is used, and misspellings and abbreviations are common. The most common

Self-proclaimed occupations among members

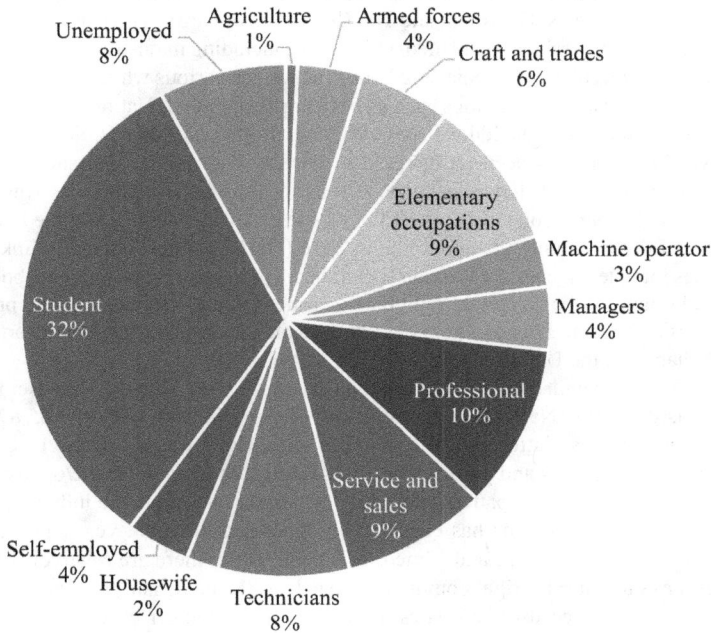

Figure 4.2 When registering, members have the option to list their occupation. This pie chart illustrates occupation categories that were manually constructed, based on the International Standard Classification of Occupations structure.

self-described occupation is "student", followed by professionals (with various IT-related professions being particularly prevalent). Various elementary occupations, such as construction and factory labor, are also common. Around 692 members report working in the military.

Analysis of the survival time (i.e., the number of years between the first and last post) and activity distribution among members indicates that most members are active for less than a year. Only 41 members have remained active for more than 15 years. Contributions to the forum are also highly unequally distributed among members, with a small number of members responsible for a large proportion of the posts.

Outlinks

An effective method of contextualizing and situating an online community within the larger online media landscape is to examine the websites to which the community predominantly links. To perform this analysis, we extracted all

URLs in all user posts. The results show that the links are primarily to various news media sites, such as BBC, DailyMail, CNN, Telegraph, New York Times, Fox News, Guardian, and Top Conservative News. There are also frequent links to various social media platforms, including mainstream platforms such as YouTube, Wikipedia, and Yahoo, as well as various white supremacist and extremist sites and blogs such as BNP.org/Britain first, Nationalvanguard. org, Amren.com, Davidduke.com, Whitecivilrights.org, and Breitbart.com. Notably, there has been an increase in links to various Russian sites since around 2008, with Kremlin-financed RT.com (previously known as Russia Today) becoming one of the most linked sites in 2015 (N:147), and the number of outlinks more than doubling in 2016 (N:317). Other frequently linked sites include Vk.com – a Russian social media platform resembling Facebook and infamous for its radical right bias, Zerohedge.com – an alt-right and pro-Russian blog, and Forza – a Russian-backed radical right party that has started a chapter in the United States.

A more detailed analysis of the top 100 sites linked in the full dataset reveals that 53% (N: 97,234) are to mainstream media sites, 36% (N: 65,877) to social media platforms, 5% (N: 9,557) to far-right media, 6% (N: 11,172) to far-right groups and parties, and 1% (N: 882) are to antagonistic/opposing groups. Although the patterns are fairly consistent over time, the influence of social media platforms has considerably increased in recent years, particularly YouTube, Reddit, and Vimeo. It is notable that there are relatively few outlinks to other far-right communities, such as 8Kun, 4Chan, Voat, and Gab. This may be because these sites tend to attract a younger crowd that often identifies themselves as alt-right activists.

Network Analysis of Members

Stormfront allows members to create "friendships" with one another, similar to the friendship functionality on Facebook. Although this feature is relatively new and used by only a fraction of the members, analyzing the friendship network as a graph enables investigation of the networks of relationships among the members. A total of 15,384 members connected by 55,163 friendship ties were identified in the analysis, although the ties were not evenly distributed among members. To focus on the elite members of the community and to make the graph more readable, members with fewer than ten friends were filtered out, resulting in a network of 581 members and 1,272 edges between them, as illustrated in Figure 4.3. This network provides a bird's-eye view of the structure of the community and reveals the most influential members in terms of formal relationships.

This network can also be used for identifying different groups within the community using a community detection algorithm (Blondel et al., 2008), which aims to identify clusters of members. The result of this analysis revealed a number of clusters in the network. By displaying the member's self-reported

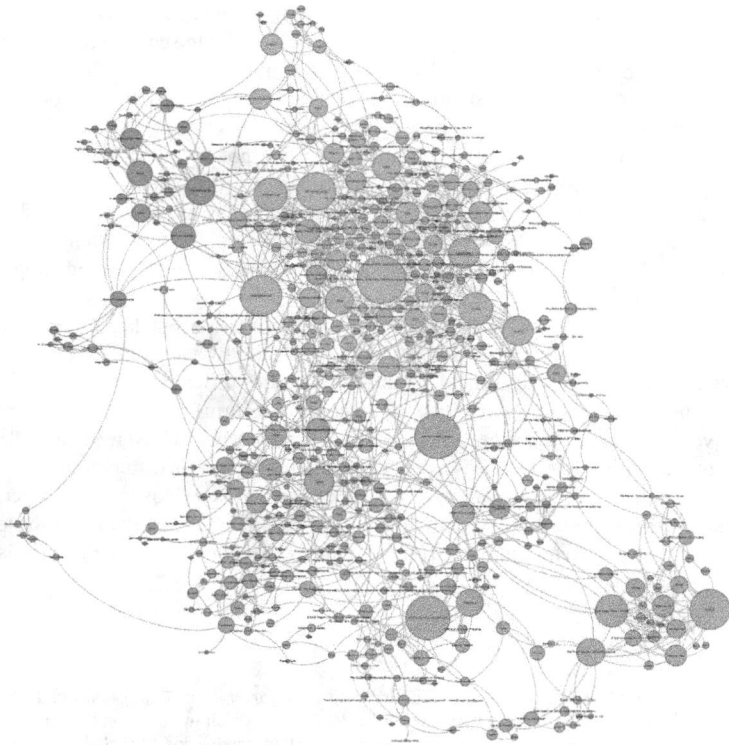

Figure 4.3 Social network analysis of the most influential members on Stormfront in terms of relationships. Node size is based on the number of mutual friendships.

geographical location as node labels, it can be observed that some of the smaller and relatively isolated clusters consist of members from particular geographical areas. This suggests that members form friendships primarily based on shared nationality. The cluster at the bottom is dominated by members from Italy, Argentina, and Brazil. The two smaller clusters at the top primarily consist of members from Ireland and the Netherlands, while the two smaller clusters to the left collect users mainly from Bulgaria and Macedonia. It should be noted that these regions also have the most active designated subforums in terms of user activity. In particular, the clusters consisting of members from the Netherlands and Italy appear relatively isolated and weakly connected to the overall network. The Italian cluster, in particular, has high internal density, indicating that these users are well-connected with each other. The likely reason for the relative isolation of these clusters is language barriers, as these subforums are more dominated by their respective language compared to other regional subforums such as England, Canada, and Australia.

However, the two largest clusters in the middle of the network are not easily explained by nationality. These clusters seem to comprise members from various countries, although many members have not specified their nationality. This suggests that there are other reasons for this clustering, such as ideological or organizational factors. While this is beyond the scope of this book, a comparative text analytic approach that compares the content of the posts by the members in each cluster could potentially identify any ideological differences.

The size of the nodes in the network represents the number of friends. The larger nodes are therefore influential and highly active members who tend to post frequently. Many of these users are "Friends of Stormfront", meaning that they provide financial support to Stormfront. Four members have particularly high scores on Betweenness Centrality, which measures the extent to which a node serves as a gatekeeper that connects different clusters. Interestingly, these users are not very active in terms of posting. However, due to ethical considerations, we do not have access to the usernames of these central members and therefore refrain from conducting any detailed analysis of these nodes.

Notes

1 We follow Mudde (2019) broad definition of the *far right* as comprising both the anti-democratic *extreme right* and the *radical right*, which includes parties that are democratic in a general sense, but against certain aspects of liberal democracy. We prefer to use the term *far right* when discussing Stormfront, since it comprises various groups and individuals on this ideological spectrum.

2 https://www.alexa.com/siteinfo/stormfront.org, and https://www.similarweb.com/website/stormfront.org#overview.

References

Beirich, H. (2014). *White homicide worldwide*. https://www.splcenter.org/sites/default/files/d6_legacy_files/downloads/publication/white-homicide-worldwide.pdf

Bliuc, A.-M., Betts, J., Vergani, M., Iqbal, M., & Dunn, K. (2019). Collective identity changes in far-right online communities: The role of offline intergroup conflict. *New media & society*, 21(8), 1770–1786. https://doi.org/10.1177/1461444819831779

Blondel, V., Guillaume, J.-L., Lambiotte, R., & Lefebvre, E. (2008). Fast unfolding of communities in large networks. *Journal of statistical mechanics: Theory experiment*, 2008(10), P10008.

Bowman-Grieve, L. (2009). Exploring "Stormfront": A virtual community of the radical right. *Studies in conflict and terrorism*, 32(11), 989–1007.

Burris, V., Smith, E., & Strahm, A. (2000). White supremacist networks on the internet. *Sociological focus*, 33(2), 215–235.

Caren, N., Jowers, K., & Gaby, S. (2012). A social movement online community: Stormfront and the white nationalist movement. In J. Earl, & D. A. Rohlinger (Eds.), *Media, movements, and political change* (pp. 63–193). Bingley: Emerald Group Publishing Limited.

Davies, G., Scrivens, R., Gaudette, T., & Frank, R. (2022). They're not all the Same: A longitudinal comparison of violent and non-violent right-wing extremist identities online. In *Right-wing extremism in Canada and the United States* (pp. 255–278). Palgrave Macmillan.

De Koster, W., & Houtman, D. (2008). 'STORMFRONT IS LIKE A SECOND HOME TO ME' On virtual community formation by right-wing extremists. *Information, communication & society*, 11(8), 1155–1176.

Hughes, E. C. (1945). Dilemmas and contradictions of status. *American journal of sociology*, 50(5), 353–359.

Kleinberg, B., van der Vegt, I., & Gill, P. (2021). The temporal evolution of a far-right forum. *Journal of computational social science*, 4, 1–23.

Lennings, C. J., Amon, K. L., Brummert, H., & Lennings, N. J. (2010). Grooming for terror: The internet and young people. *Psychiatry, psychology and law*, 17(3), 424–437.

Mudde, C. (2019). *The far right today*. Cambridge: Polity.

Perry, B., & Scrivens, R. (2016). White pride worldwide: Constructing global identities online. In J. Schweppe, & M. Walters (Eds.), *The globalisation of hate: Internationalising hate crime* (pp. 65–78). New York: Oxford University Press.

SÄPO. (2021). *Säkerhetspolisens årsrapport 2021*. https://sakerhetspolisen.se/down load/18.650ed51617f9c29b552287/1649683389251/Sakerhetspolisen_arsbok%20 2021.pdf

Scrivens, R., Davies, G., & Frank, R. (2020). Measuring the evolution of radical right-wing posting behaviors online. *Deviant behavior*, 41(2), 216–232.

Simi, P., & Futrell, R. (2009). Negotiating white power activist stigma. *Social problems*, 56(1), 89–110.

Simi, P., & Futrell, R. (2015). *American Swastika: Inside the white power movement's hidden spaces of hate*. London: Rowman & Littlefield.

U.S. Department of Justice, U. S. D. o. H. a. H. S. (2022). *Raising awareness of hate crimes and hate incidents during the COVID-19 pandemic*. https://www.justice.gov/ file/1507346/download

Wong, M. A., Frank, R., & Allsup, R. (2015). The supremacy of online white supremacists—An analysis of online discussions by white supremacists. *Information & communications technology law*, 24(1), 41–73.

5 Identity

Becoming a Community[1]

The Durkheimian perspective focuses on identity, as rituals are said to foster a sense of shared identity among the participants. As individuals come to see themselves in others, this leads to a common understanding of "we", or seeing the "we" in "me" (Cohen, 1985; Melucci, 1989; Touraine, 1985). Such a shared sense of identity is considered the basis for collective action.

The influence of social media on identity has been a focus of academic attention since the inception of the internet. The internet provides a platform for individuals with even the most obscure and fringe interests to connect and build communities around their shared passion. Extensive literature on media has suggested that engagement with such communities influences our sense of self. Online communities seem capable of transforming shared interests into fledging identities. An initial curiosity in anime cosplaying, for example, may lead us to join an online community focused on this interest. Over time, our social network becomes increasingly based on these interactions, leading to self-identification as an anime cosplayer. We adopt specific attire, learn a particular vernacular, and experience a sense of allegiance and belonging to the community, seeing ourselves as *different* from mainstream culture and perhaps considering ourselves superior in certain aspects. Research has suggested that such strengthening of identity can positively affect members of minority groups by fostering a sense of sense of belonging (Lloyd, 2014). However, it can have more complex and potentially problematic implications when it comes to political life.

The Durkheimian emphasis on identity and rituals suggests an alternative approach to politics, one rooted in group identity rather than opinions and arguments. This identity-centric approach resonates both with an emerging understanding of the nature of contemporary polarization within the political science literature and with long-established social movement research that casts radicalization as a form of socialization.

Political science has, in recent years, increasingly emphasized the role of identity in political life. For instance, Miller and Conover (2015) state that "the behavior of partisans resembles that of sports team members acting to preserve the status of their teams rather than thoughtful citizens participating in the political process for the broader good" (p. 225). They argue that what drives

DOI: 10.4324/9781003108344-6

individuals to participate and engage in politics is not policies or a political agenda but identity; "When partisans endure meetings, plant yard signs, write checks, and spend endless hours volunteering, what is likely foremost in their minds is that they are furious with the opposing party and want intensely to avoid losing to it – not a specific issue agenda. They are fired-up team members on a mission to defeat the other team". Likewise, in their influential book, political scientists Achen and Bartels (2017) argue that "voting behavior is primarily a product of inherited partisan loyalties, social identities and symbolic attachments. Over time, engaged citizens may construct policy preferences and ideologies that rationalize their choices, but those issues are seldom fundamental".

This literature emerged from the observation of a substantial rise in partisan aversion in the US in recent decades, while issue-position polarization has remained fixed and relatively low, thus suggesting that a novel form of polarization is at play (Fiorina, 2017). This form of polarization has been termed "affective" (Iyengar, Sood & Lelkes, 2012), "sectarian" (Finkel et al., 2020), or "social" polarization (Mason, 2018), suggesting that it is propelled by deeply rooted mechanisms of group affiliation in human psychology (Iyengar et al., 2019). By forging a politics founded on out-group aversion rather than political ideals, this identity-centered polarization transforms elections from contests over policy disagreements into struggles between warring tribes, separated by a fundamental sense of difference (Sides, Tesler & Vavreck, 2018). Sectarian polarization transforms issue positions into symbols of group belonging, implying that while changes in issue position may occur as a result of radicalization, they are secondary to a process of socialization (Törnberg et al., 2021). While social identity has always played a role in politics, this body of literature suggests that we have entered a situation in which partisan identity is coming to dominate or even engulf other identities (Iyengar et al., 2012, 2019; Klein, 2020).

Identity has also been given a central stage in research on radicalization and extremist movements, where it is seen as a key component in the "increased preparation for and commitment to intergroup conflict" (McCauley & Moskalenko, 2008, p. 416). A long tradition of radicalization understands it as a process of individuals joining and, over time, becoming subsumed into communities, coming to view themselves as a part of a larger collective, often defined through its opposition against an external group (Borum, 2011a, 2011b; Della Porta, 2013; Sageman, 2008). Through this lens, to be radicalized means to have one's political identity as dominant in one's self-understanding.

The social movement literature uses the notion of "collective identity" to refer to the role of identity in movements, suggesting that such collective identities are constructed as activists interact and share ideas with other members of their in-group (Futrell & Simi, 2004; Polletta & Jasper, 2001). Recent studies have argued that social movements can also make use of social media for such identity work, using digital messages to develop a common sense of "we" (Gaudette et al., 2021). The focus on social identity resonates with research in social media studies, which has gathered significant evidence to suggest that social media have become a site for the formation of identities (Van Haperen, Uitermark & Van der Zeeuw, 2020) and are capable of fostering communities with a strong sense of group solidarity (Beyer, 2014; Crossley, 2015; Papacharissi, 2010; Turkle, 2011).

In this chapter, we suggest that online spaces like Stormfront constitute central loci for the formation of such collective identities. We draw on the Durkheimian framework to argue that what takes place in these types of spaces can be best understood as the development of collective identities through the elaboration of a cultural and discursive system. As individuals come together in a digital space under the banner of a shared interest, this interest tends to be transformed into a collective identity, simultaneously articulated into a discourse that serves to separate insiders from outsiders and function as linguistic capital within the community (Bourdieu, 1991). Following the literature on discursive identity, their collectivity and subjectivity are *contained* within these discourses (Benwell, 2006; Wodak, De Cillia & Reisigl, 1999).

To examine the effects on individual identity of participating in the community, we view identity through the lens of discourse and trace language evolution as users engage with the community (Danescu-Niculescu-Mizil et al., 2013; Kleinberg, van der Vegt & Mozes, 2020). Focusing on individual radicalization and member recruitment, we trace the evolution of the language of new members as they become part of the community, and we use the contrast between new and old users to draw out the linguistic expressions of community belonging and intersubjectivity that is, of members' sense of "we-ness".

Durkheim on Community and Rituals

In media studies, an important focus of research on fringe online space has been their capacity to drive discursive and cultural processes, examining how web culture has grown to become a radicalizing political force (Belew, 2018; Nagle, 2017; Reagle, 2015). This literature has found that digital spaces appear to have an innate tendency to produce rich internal subcultures – involving particular vernaculars, slang, memes, and stories (Zannettou et al., 2018). In the early period of the internet, these mostly consisted of harmless jokes and cultural expressions, such as taking cute pictures of breaded cats or unexpected appearances in the music video for the 1987 hit song "Never Gonna Give You Up".

In more recent years, however, the cultural expressions emerging from these fringe spaces have taken on a political and distinctly reactionary hue. This period has seen a constant flow of extremist discourses, ideas, and memes from fringe online spaces into the political mainstream, which has contributed to the mainstreaming of White supremacist ideology – ranging from novel hate symbols, such as Pepe the Frog or the OK hand signal, to far-right conspiracies such as the Great Replacement or QAnon. As this culture has become political, these spaces' remarkable capacity for discursive innovation, memes, slang, and stories through constant playful experimentation has made them a real political force. As scholars have argued, these memes and stories encode certain political subjectivities constructed around a vague notion of a shared "other", which can function to drive political conflict (DeCook, 2018; Tuters & Hagen, 2020).

In this chapter, we use our Durkheimian lens to understand how communities and social identities are formed. As discussed in Chapter 2, the Durkheimian perspective suggests that social membership, moral beliefs, and cultural production are linked together by the same mechanism: ideas are symbols of group membership, and culture is thus generated by the emotional patterns of social interaction within religious rituals. The process of community formation links social membership, moral beliefs, and cultural production through a single mechanism: ideas are symbols of group membership, and culture is thus generated by the emotional patterns of social interaction within religious rituals. We can examine the emergence of an internal culture as inextricably interlinked with the strengthening of a collective political identity.

We will use this Durkheimian theory for community formation to empirically study the exchange of messages. We focus on the linguistic evolution of members as they, over time, become socialized into the community. To examine the members' language over time, we compare members' early posts with their later posts in order to examine how the language of posts changes over time as members engage with the community. Focusing on individual radicalization and member recruitment, we trace the evolution of the language of new members as they become part of the community and use the contrast between new and old members to draw out the particularities of the community discourse.[2]

Language Convergence

We begin with the simple question of the distance between newly joined members and the forum's overall language, to examine how user language shifts over time as members engage with the community.

Central to discursive community formation is the idea that communities tend to develop an internal culture built through sustained, low-intensity exchange of messages, in which particular ideas, words, stories, and beliefs come to symbolize membership and connection to the community. The words signal to belong, and learning this internal language is thus central to becoming part of the community and successfully participating in its discursive rituals. This suggests that users who enter the community need to learn this community language and that learning this culture is necessary to attain the emotional energy that drives users to continue their participation. This, in turn, can be seen as users converging on the community language, coming to take up the discourse, themes, and stories of the community.

To measure the distance between members and the community overall, we construct a language model that represents the forum's overall language by selecting a random sample consisting of 20,000 messages. To measure the distance between two corpora, we use bag-of-words representations, that is, we capture the frequency of each word used. To capture the distance between two such bags of words, we use cosine similarity, which looks at how similar or different the frequency of words used are.

We first look at the cosine distance – a measure of the similarity of the language used – between new members and the community as a function of how many posts they have contributed. As we want to follow the same members over a longer time to see how their language use evolves, we focus on members who have sent at least 50 posts since this selection effectively captures highly active long-term members.

To examine whether users indeed converge with the language of the community, we looked at the cosine distance between new members and the community as a function of how many posts they have contributed. Figure 5.1 shows the convergence of users by their post number.

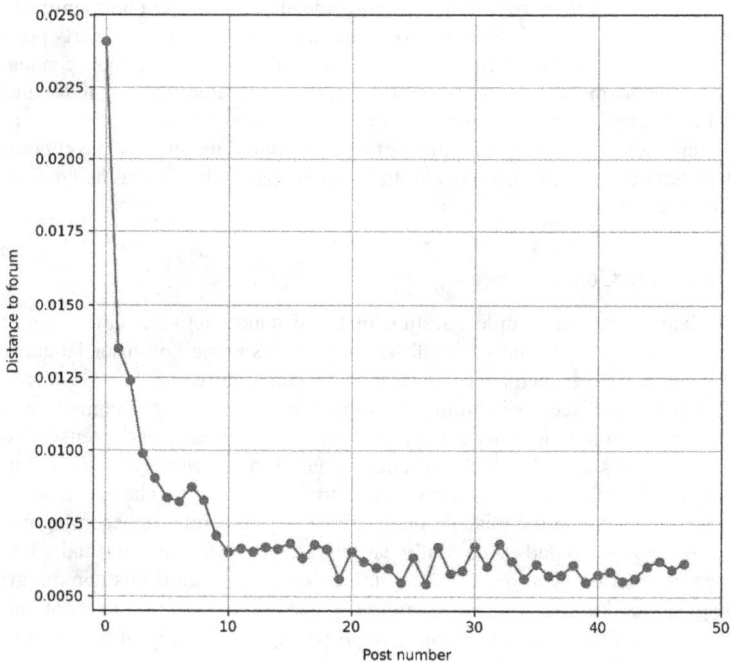

Figure 5.1 This figure displays the cosine distance between members' posts, in posting order, and the overall community language over time. As depicted, new members quickly converge with the forum discourse.

The results are quite striking. The members begin far from the forum language but relatively quickly converge as they engage with the community. After about 20 posts, almost complete convergence has taken place. This suggests that members quickly absorb the defining discourse of the community.

Members who fail to take up the language should furthermore be expected to be more likely to leave the community, as successful participation in conversation rituals requires adopting the community discourse. To see this, we compared the posts of the members who stayed with those who did not to see the extent to which their posts differ. We looked at members who posted only a few messages and compared their trajectories with members who became long-term contributors.

To see this, we compare the posts of the members who stayed with those who did not, to see the extent to which their posts differ. We look at members who posted only a few messages and compare their trajectories with the members who became long-term members. Figure 5.2 shows the result.

As the figure illustrates, the members who only remain for a few posts are significantly further away from the forum's mainstream discourse in the initial posts than the members who become long-term members. It takes about five posts for the short-term members to reach the place where the long-term members begin in their first posts. After this, these members appear to cease their converge with the forum language, instead moving further away before leaving the forum.

Content of Lexical Change

A second central idea of discursive community formation is that the language of the community contains within it a worldview. Studying the discourse of a community can, therefore, throw light on the ideology of the community – their definitions of good and evil. To do so, we must examine what is characteristic of the community's language – what changes in the member's language as they converge with the community? What are the differences in language between new members and long-term members? What are the words that reveal socialization?

To examine this, we inductively compare members' early posts and later posts. To do so, we use Log-Likelihood to identify the most overrepresented words in the early posts compared to the overall community posts. This allows us to find words and bigrams that are statistically over- and underrepresented in the community language – words that have come to function as membership emblems.

We create two subcorpora based on posts from members who have written at least 50 posts. The first consists of posts 1–20, and the second consists of post 30 to 50. This selection allows seeing the language before and after the members have converged on the forum language and is selected such that the corpora have a similar number of words. This allows us to inductively

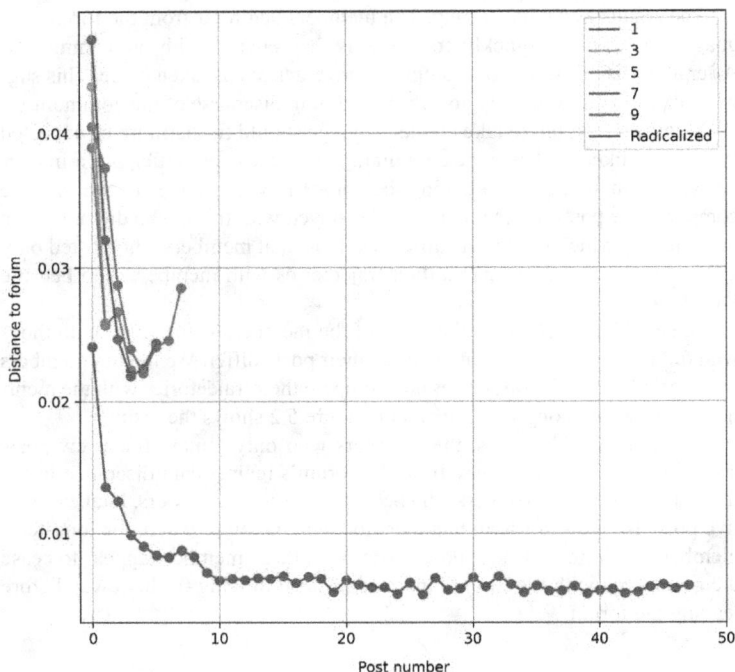

Figure 5.2 This figure illustrates the cosine distance between members' posts, in posting order, and the overall community language over time. The numbers
indicate the total posts written by users before they leave the forum. For
example, '3' denotes users who have written three posts before their de-
parture. The figure reveals that new members quickly align with the forum
discourse. Notably, members who leave after a fewer number of posts start
with a greater distance from the forum language and tend to diverge further
in their final posts before leaving.

identify words and bigrams that are statistically over- and underrepresented
in the community language; that is, the words that have come to function as
membership emblems.

Figure 5.3 shows the most overrepresented words of the two corpora as
two word clouds. This shows that the vocabulary shifts from a focus on pronouns like "my" and "I" to "you" and "your", suggesting that members focus
less on themselves and more on the community. There is furthermore a shift
from "white" and "blacks" to "wn" (for "White Nationalist") and "Jews",
indicating a shift in the focus ingroup and outgroup. However, a limitation
of the Log-Likelihood approach is that it does not distinguish between jargon
changes and thematic changes: some of the shifts reflect changing ways of

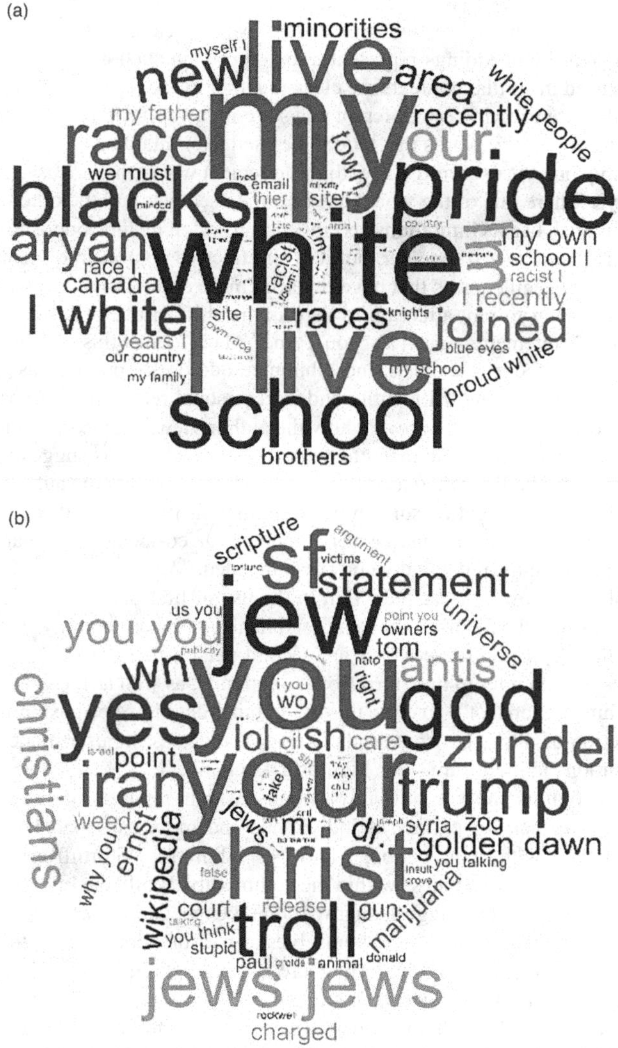

(a)

(b)

Figure 5.3 The top figure (a) shows the most Log-Likelihood overrepresented words among new members, and the bottom figure (b) among the established members. Unlike traditional word clouds where word size is proportional to frequency, here the size represents the Log-Likelihood overrepresentation of the word. The included words are from the top-5000 list of the most common words in both corpora. The clouds include bigrams, meaning some words are repeated. The corpora contain a total of 5,937,177 tokens.

referring to the same issue, while others reflect a change in the issues discussed. To separate these two, we can use what is called word embedding models. Word embeddings represent a text corpus in such a way that words that are used in similar contexts are close together in the representation, while words that are used in very different ways are far away from each other. This allows us to identify words that tend to be used in similar ways.

Simply put, we use word embeddings to look at words that are used in similar ways, where one of the words has become used less and the other more.[3] This approach has its limitations, as embeddings often include opposite words or words that are used together, but it is an effective approach to identifying community-specific terms that have replaced more commonly used words.

A first thing to pay attention to here is the shift in use of pronouns and "indexical" statements – such as "you", "me", "here", and "this" – which both scholars of discourse analysis and ethnomethodologists point to as an important site through which identity and interpersonal relations are expressed. The use of these words can reveal how the author views themselves and their relationship with their audience: the word "I", for instance, is suggestive of a sense of individuality, whereas the use of "we" suggests that the author views themselves as representing something larger than themselves. Indexical terms are also indicative of a sense of being situated or co-located in a particular setting in which meaning and value are embedded.

Table 5.1 shows a clear reduction in the use of first-person singular ("I", "my", "Im") as the members become established in the community. Table 5.1 shows that replacing these words are second-person plural ("you", "your"), which is used to refer to the Stormfront community, as well as the word "wn", for "White Nationalist". To draw this out in more detail, we can examine how the fraction of posts that contain the words changes as the user makes more contributions to the forum – see Figures 5.4 and 5.5.

These figures show a shift in pronouns, which suggests that the members refer to themselves less as individuals and more as situated within a community – with "you", "your", and "sf" (short for "Stormfront") being used to mark the situatedness within the community. While the literature (e.g. DiMaggio et al. 2018) suggests that we should expect an increase of "we" or "us" as individuals come to see themselves as part of a community, this does not appear to be the case. Similarly, there is only a slight increase in the use of "they"/"them". This suggests that members do not write as if representing the community – through an inclusive "we" – but rather as if *addressing* the community – an inclusive "you" or "sf".

Another interesting shift that occurs over time is that from mainstream terms to community-specific jargon and themes, which function as markers of community belonging and contain within them the white supremacist ideology of the forum. Figure 5.5 (and also Table 5.1) shows a number of such community-specific terms. Examples of such community-specific vernacular that are rarely used in mainstream discourse are "anti-white" and "white genocide", which

Table 5.1 This table illustrates the evolution of word usage with similar meaning as members become more established in the community.

	Replacement words
my	your
I	you, lol, they
white	nonwhite
myself	you, wn
blacks	groids, they, negroes, nigs
black	groid, negro, nonwhite
I'm	you, lol
our	your
aryan	aryanism
minorities	they
site	sf, blog
slavic	uralic
hey	lol, yeah, haha, yea, kidding, nah
dislike	think, disagree
feel	think
I've	Sf
government	zog
edl	uaf, efp
media	msm, zog
information	evidence
turks	armenians, azeris, tatars
wp	wn
movement	party, wn, wnism
guys	guy, lol, you, haha
people	they, wns
politically	morally
replies	comments, comment
caucasian	australoid, arabids
enemy	zog

Note. Replacement words are selected by their Log-Likelihood overrepresentation, multiplied by their word embedding similarity, with a minimum threshold of 5 for inclusion. Words without any new words replacements are excluded.

emphasize the community's ideological starting point of white people being the true victims of racism. Another example is the replacement of "government" for "zog" – short for "Zionist Occupational Government", referring to an antisemitic conspiracy theory claiming Jews secretly control Western governments. "Media" is similarly replaced with "msm" ("mainstream media") or, again, with "zog".

The community-specific vernacular contains within it the ideology of the forum. For instance, the use of "negroid" reference historic race theory, suggesting that humankind can be divided into different races. A similar shift can be seen in references used for a number of national and ethnic groups, where Stormfront members, over time, learn to emphasize ethnicity over nationality

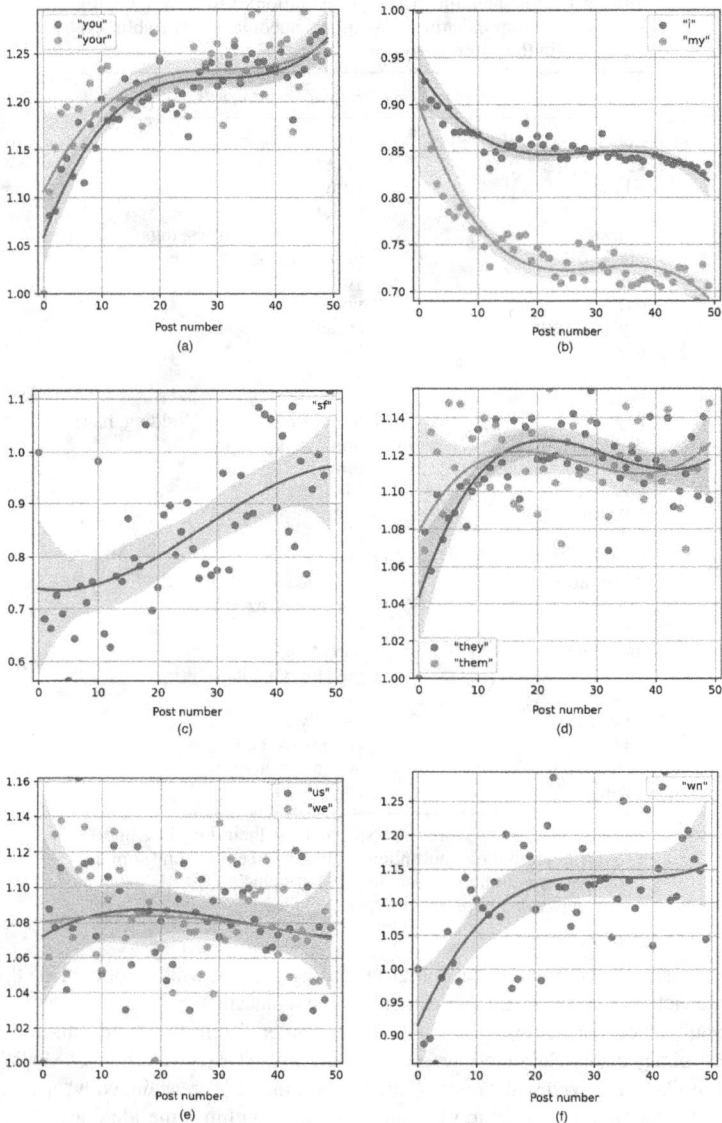

Figure 5.4 These graphs (a–f) display the fraction of words in the first, second, third, etc., posts of members who write at least 50 posts. The data is normalized by the fraction of words in the first message to show the relative increase or decrease. An order-3 polynomial linear regression model with a 0.95 confidence interval was used to estimate the data.

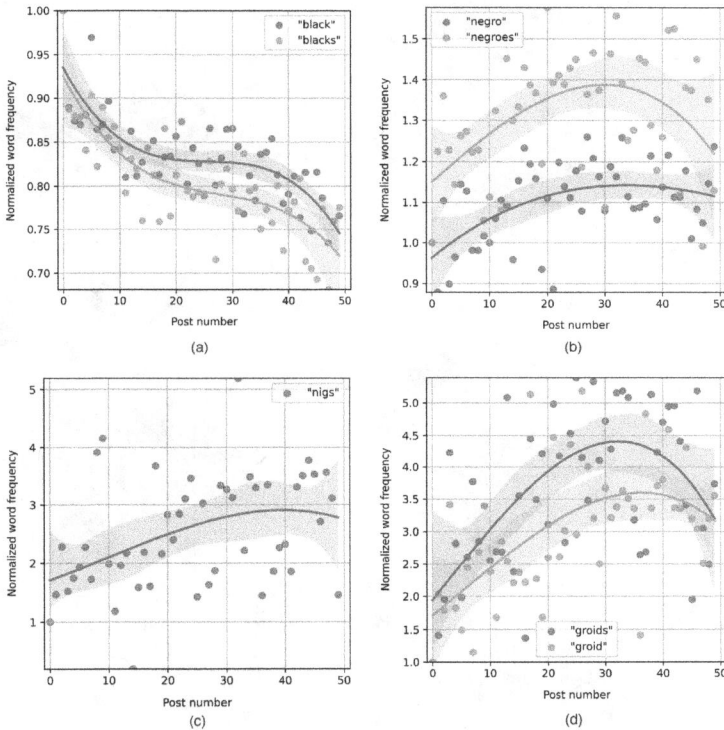

Figure 5.5 These graphs (a–d) illustrate the shift from the terms "black"/"blacks" to community-specific jargon within the forum. As members become more engaged, the frequency of "black"/"blacks" noticeably decreases. Part of this decline is due to a thematic shift in focus toward Jews as the outgroup, reflecting the forum's strong anti-Semitic tendencies. However, as Table 1 indicates, these terms are also replaced with community-specific terms like "negroes", "groids", or "nigs" (it is important to note that the forum prohibits the use of the more common racist N-word).

and race over ethnicity, often drawing on historic race theory terms. For instance, "turks" are replaced by "armenians", "azeris", "tatars", that is, ethnic groups living in Turkey. Similarly, "white" and "caucasian" both fall in use, being replaced by "australoids" and "arabids". "Australoid" was a race theoretic term for people of Australia, Melanesia, and parts of Southeast Asia, whereas "Arabids" was used to capture a racial division between peoples of Semitic ethnicities and peoples of other ethnicities. These terms thus serve the particular function of separating Jewish people from the larger group of white people, suggesting that they constitute a separate race.

Finally, we can look at shifting words that may capture the emotional energy experienced by participants of successful rituals. Emotional energy is

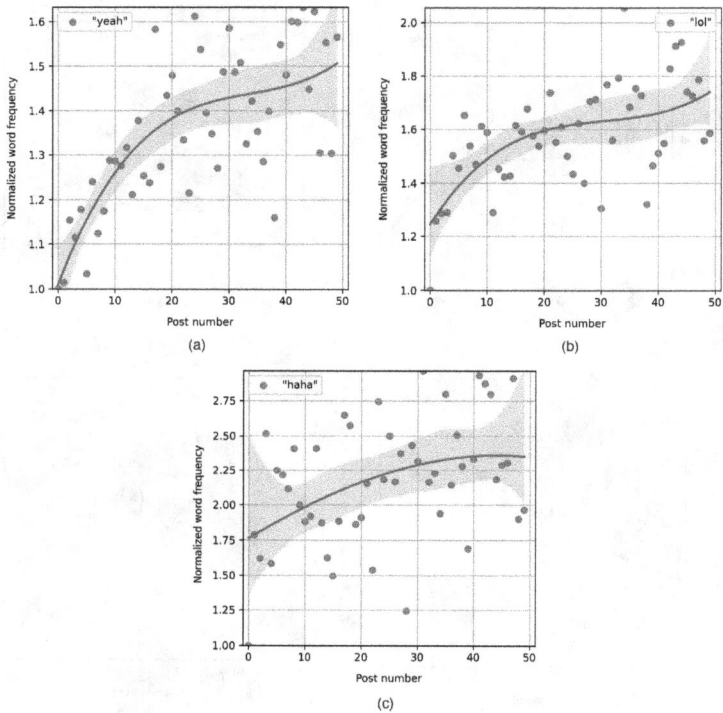

Figure 5.6 These figures (a–c) explore the change in words that signal emotional energy, "yeah", "lol", and "haha". These all increase as members engage with the community. Tendency lines approximated by order-3 polynomial linear regression model with 0.95 confidence interval.

difficult to capture in data, as it is not necessarily linked to a positive tonality – emotional energy can also be found in a shared sense of outrage or anger. However, a simple way of tracing emotional energy is by linguistic markers signifying relaxed interaction, for instance, words like "lol", "haha", and "yeah". As Figure 5.6 shows, these words increase significantly as a member engages with the community, suggesting that members become more relaxed and that they draw emotional energy from the interaction.

Conclusion

This chapter has examined how individuals' identities are affected by their participation and engagement with the Stormfront community. The chapter has used text analysis to empirically employ the Durkheimian lens on the Stormfront community – starting from the notion that fringe online spaces such as Stormfront provide spaces for repeated conversation rituals, which instills individuals with a sense of social membership and intersubjectivity, while at the same time producing a distinct internal culture.

The empirical analysis confirmed that users quickly converge with the overall discourse of the community – they absorb its shared reality. As they acquire the language of the community, they absorb its symbols and employ these to perform storytelling about themselves, thus creating links between their personal identity and the community (Danescu-Niculescu-Mizil et al., 2013; Kleinberg, van der Vegt & Gill, 2021). The stories we tell about ourselves, our role in the world, and our link to our community are simultaneously stories about the world which guide our actions.

This may also help explain the often strange and esoteric vernaculars and subcultures of internet communities that have long been observed by digital media scholars. As social media provides only these means of expression and communication, discourse and language become the central locus of defining the community and demarking it from the outside world. The rituals produce a feeling of intersubjectivity while at the same time filling particular stories, styles, jargon, and topics of conversation with membership significance. Community-building is, in this sense, a discursive process: languages are the way the community "reifies its experience, makes it thing-like, and thus an emblem, treated as having noun-like permanence" (Collins 2004:37). Beliefs, words, and ideas come to function as sacred group symbols, filled with a sense of group membership. The result is that the cultural and discursive worlds in which we operate become increasingly an expression of the groups to which we belong.

The language of the community is intertwined with its view of the world: what is good and what is evil. The production of a group is necessarily also the creation of difference; as Benhabib (1996:33) puts it, "every search for identity includes differentiating oneself from what one is not" – identifying the in-group with good and evil as what is outside the group's boundary. In the Durkheimian perspective, conflict and violence occur as a result of this process, as we come to see ourselves as completely virtuous and our enemy as completely evil, which means that anything we do to the outgroup will be legitimate. Violence and conflict are not the opposite of social cooperation and solidarity but rather the other side of the same coin.

The Durkheimian perspective links beliefs and stories that instantiate political subjectivities to our social identity; such beliefs and stories thereby become sacred, functioning as links between us and our community, and are, therefore, part of that which is taken for granted and beyond question. Such sacred beliefs have, in recent years, received significant scholarly attention within social psychology, which has shown how various deep-rooted psychological mechanisms protect these beliefs from being challenged (Kahan, 2017). Our identities shape our cognition through mechanisms such as "confirmation bias", "deductive", and "motivated reasoning" – in which our objective judgment and our rationality are affected by our identities and interests (Nickerson, 1998; Wood & Porter, 2019). This type of "Identity-Protective Cognition" (Kahan, 2017) is understood as a way of avoiding dissonance and estrangement from one's social group by subconsciously resisting any information that threatens the group's defining values. In short, such sacred ideas are not fully subject to rational interrogation, as they operate in the realm of social identity rather than that of rational deliberation. Discursive community formation suggests that social media platforms naturally lead to the elaboration of such sacred ideas, thus suggesting a potential link between fringe digital spaces and the rise of misinformation.

The suggestion is thus that social media – and fringe spaces like Stormfront in particular – are reshaping politics by acting on our identities. As social media allow us to meet with like-minded individuals under the banner of a shared interest, these meeting spaces, over time, produce collective identities. The much-observed playful linguistic innovation that characterizes these communities fulfills the function of demarcating community boundaries and defining linguistic capital within the community.

For white supremacist communities like Stormfront, the Durkheimian perspective describes online radicalization as a form of socialization: individuals become subsumed in a community, which grows in importance to such an extent that they are willing to hurt and be hurt for it. In this sense, the notion of "online self-radicalization" is misleading: these online spaces are profoundly social, and the process of online radicalization is very much a process of socialization.

Notes

1 An earlier version of this chapter was published as "Inside a White Power echo chamber: Why fringe digital spaces are polarizing politics", in *New Media & Society*, https://doi.org/10.1177/14614448221122915 Reprinted by permission of Sage Journals.

2 For pre-processing the corpus, we identify language of the posts using the Python package langdetect, and focus on the English-language posts ($N = 8{,}806{,}105$) that are over 120 characters long ($N = 6{,}158{,}005$, from 81,039 members). We also truncate messages at the closest whitespace character preceding the 5,000th character, to prevent a small number of extremely long messages from distorting the results (these messages are often copies of reports or lists of data, such as a 314,743-character post listing the purported prices of body parts on the Egyptian organ market).

3 We created a word embedding model (word2vec) of the combined materials of the early and late posts of the members. We then look at the most overrepresented words in one corpus, and compare with the most similar, and most underrepresented words in the other corpus. We focus on the top-300 most overrepresented words of the 5000 most used words. For each of these words, we look at the top-20 words that are closest in embedding space, and multiply their similarity score in the embedding (that is, how close they are in the vector space, from 0 to 1) with the Log Likelihood-score that shows how much the word has increase in use in later messages.

References

Achen, C. H., & Bartels, L. M. (2017). *Democracy for realists*. Princeton: Princeton University Press.

Belew, K. (2018). *Bring the war home*. Boston: Harvard University Press.

Benhabib, S. (1996). *Democracy and difference: Contesting the boundaries of the political*. New York: Princeton University Press.

Benwell, B. (2006). *Discourse and identity*. Edinburgh: Edinburgh University Press.

Beyer, J. L. (2014). *Expect us: Online communities and political mobilization*. London: Oxford University Press.

Borum, R. (2011a). Radicalization into violent extremism I: A review of social science theories. *Journal of strategic security*, 4(4), 7–36.

Borum, R. (2011b). Rethinking radicalization. *Journal of strategic security*, 4(4), 1–6.

Bourdieu, P. (1991). *Language and symbolic power*. Boston: Harvard University Press.

Cohen, J. (1985). Strategy or identity: New theoretical paradigms and contemporary social movements. *Social research*, 52(4). 663–716.

Collins, R. (2004). *Interaction ritual chains*. Princeton: Princeton University Press.

Crossley, A. D. (2015). Facebook feminism: Social media, blogs, and new technologies of contemporary US feminism. *Mobilization: An international quarterly*, 20(2), 253–268.

Danescu-Niculescu-Mizil, C., West, R., Jurafsky, D., Leskovec, J., & Potts, C. (2013). *No country for old members: User lifecycle and linguistic change in online communities*. Paper presented at the Proceedings of the 22nd international conference on World Wide Web.

DeCook, J. R. (2018). Memes and symbolic violence:# proudboys and the use of memes for propaganda and the construction of collective identity. *Learning, media and technology*, 43(4), 485–504.

Della Porta, D. (2013). *Clandestine political violence*. Cambridge: Cambridge University Press.

DiMaggio, P., Bernier, C., Heckscher, C., et al. (2018). Interaction ritual threads: Does IRC theory apply online? In E. B. Weininger, L. Annette, & O. Lizardo (Eds.), *Ritual, emotion, violence: Studies on the micro-sociology of Randall Collins* (pp. 81–124). London: Taylor & Francis.

Finkel, E. J., Bail, C. A., Cikara, M., Ditto, P. H., Iyengar, S., Klar, S., & Rand, D. G. (2020). Political sectarianism in America. *Science*, 370(6516), 533–536.

Fiorina, M. P. (2017). *Unstable majorities: Polarization, party sorting, and political stalemate*. New York: Hoover Press.

Futrell, R., & Simi, P. (2004). Free spaces, collective identity, and the persistence of US white power activism. *Social problems*, 51(1), 16–42.

Gaudette, T., Scrivens, R., Davies, G., & Frank, R. (2021). Upvoting extremism: Collective identity formation and the extreme right on Reddit. *New media & society*, 23(12), 3491–3508.

Iyengar, S., Lelkes, Y., Levendusky, M., Malhotra, N., & Westwood, S. J. (2019). The origins and consequences of affective polarization in the United States. *Annual review of political science*, 22, 129–146.

Iyengar, S., Sood, G., & Lelkes, Y. (2012). Affect, not ideology: A social identity perspective on polarization. *Public opinion quarterly*, 76(3), 405–431.

Kahan, D. M. (2017). Misconceptions, misinformation, and the logic of identity-protective cognition. Cultural cognition project working paper series no. 164. https://papers.ssrn.com/sol3/papers.cfm?abstract_id=2973067

Klein, E. (2020). *Why we're polarized.* New York: Simon and Schuster.

Kleinberg, B., van der Vegt, I., & Gill, P. (2021). The temporal evolution of a far-right forum. *Journal of computational social science,* 4, 1–23.

Kleinberg, B., van der Vegt, I., & Mozes, M. (2020). Measuring emotions in the COVID-19 real world worry dataset. *arXiv preprint arXiv:2004.04225.*

Lloyd, A. (2014). Social media, help or hindrance: What role does social media play in young people's mental health? *Psychiatria danubina,* 26(suppl 1), 340–346.

Mason, L. (2018). Losing common ground: Social sorting and polarization. *The Forum,* 16(1), pp. 47–66.

McCauley, C., & Moskalenko, S. (2008). Mechanisms of political radicalization: Pathways toward terrorism. *Terrorism and political violence,* 20(3), 415–433.

Melucci, A. (1989). *Nomads of the present: Social movements and individual needs in contemporary society.* New York: Vintage.

Miller, P. R., & Conover, P. J. (2015). Red and blue states of mind: Partisan hostility and voting in the United States. *Political research quarterly,* 68(2), 225–239.

Nagle, A. (2017). *Kill all normies: Online culture wars from 4Chan and Tumblr to Trump and the Alt-Right.* Alresford: Zero Books.

Nickerson, R. S. (1998). Confirmation bias: A ubiquitous phenomenon in many guises. *Review of general psychology,* 2(2), 175–220.

Papacharissi, Z. (2010). *A networked self: Identity, community, and culture on social network sites.* New York: Routledge.

Polletta, F., & Jasper, J. M. (2001). Collective identity and social movements. *Annual review of sociology,* 27(1), 283–305.

Reagle, J. M. (2015). *Reading the comments: Likers, haters, and manipulators at the bottom of the web.* Boston: MIT Press.

Sageman, M. (2008). The next generation of terror. *Foreign policy,* 165, 37. https://foreignpolicy.com/2009/10/08/the-next-generation-of-terror/

Sides, J., Tesler, M., & Vavreck, L. (2018). *Identity crisis: The 2016 presidential campaign and the battle for the meaning of America.* New York: Princeton University Press.

Törnberg, P., Andersson, C., Lindgren, K., & Banisch, S. (2021). Modeling the emergence of affective polarization in the social media society. *PloS one,* 16(10), e0258259.

Touraine, A. (1985). An introduction to the study of social movements. *Social research,* 52(4). 749–787.

Turkle, S. (2011). *Life on the screen.* New York: Simon and Schuster.

Tuters, M., & Hagen, S. (2020). (((They))) rule: Memetic antagonism and nebulous othering on 4chan. *New media & society,* 22(12), 2218–2237.

Van Haperen, S., Uitermark, J., & Van der Zeeuw, A. (2020). Mediated interaction rituals: A geography of everyday life and contention in Black Lives Matter. *Mobilization: An international quarterly,* 25(3), 295–313.

Wodak, R., De Cillia, R., & Reisigl, M. (1999). The discursive construction of national identities. *Discourse and society,* 10(2), 149–173.

Wood, T., & Porter, E. (2019). The elusive backfire effect: Mass attitudes' steadfast factual adherence. *Political behavior,* 41, 135–163.

Zannettou, S., Caulfield, T., Blackburn, J., De Cristofaro, E., Sirivianos, M., Stringhini, G., & Suarez-Tangil, G. (2018). *On the origins of memes by means of fringe web communities.* Paper presented at the Proceedings of the internet measurement conference 2018.

6 Discourse

Constructing a Worldview[1]

As we have seen, in the Durkheimian perspective, words and stories can function as markers of community belonging – they define the boundaries of the community and separate insiders from outsiders. But these stories are not *only* expressions of community belonging and shared identity; they are also ways of making sense of the world. They constitute a particular worldview intimately intertwined with the community identity. These stories ultimately determine how the members of the community act, by identifying problems and suggesting solutions, and thus create opportunities for action.

The internet has been associated with a rapid decline in the quality and credibility of information: while the internet was initially hailed as an unprecedented source of easily accessible knowledge, it has paradoxically been associated with the rise of biased narratives, "fake news", conspiracy theories, mistrust, and paranoia. The digital world seems to provide fertile soil for the growth of misinformation, as studies show that false news diffuses faster, farther, and deeper than true news in social networks (Vosoughi, Roy & Aral, 2018). The rise of misinformation is now seen as a major threat to public safety and modern democracy (Howell, 2013; Poushter, Fagan & Gubbala, 2022).

Researchers have suggested a possible link between online spaces and the growing spread of misinformation, as homogeneous clusters of users with a preference for self-confirmation seem to provide capable greenhouses for the seedlings of rumors and misinformation (Törnberg, 2018). As we have seen, the traditional echo chamber hypothesis – built on the Habermasian idea of public deliberation – suggests that these spaces bring about such worldviews through a process of one-sided rational discussion. People are exposed only to information and opinions that reinforce their existing beliefs, and they are shielded from different perspectives or dissenting views. In such an environment, participants are said to develop false understandings of the world as they fail to consider considering alternative viewpoints. If narratives remain unchallenged by counternarratives, it is presumed they can withstand rational deliberation despite being fundamentally flawed. Communities are thus said to build worldviews from

DOI: 10.4324/9781003108344-7

their distinct assumptions and values, which are rational and internally coherent – but ultimately based on false presumptions.

However, the Durkheimian perspective – and the previous chapters of this book – hint at an alternative mechanism that may link online communities and the rise of misinformation. Communities may develop a shared worldview not through aloof rational deliberation and evaluation of competing arguments but through a Durkheimian process that is inextricably part of community formation and belonging.

In this chapter, we will seek to elaborate on this Durkheimian understanding of how communities build shared worldviews. We will do so by analyzing the collective, bottom-up processes through which members of Stormfront made sense of two key events in the forum's history: the election of Obama in 2008 and the election of Trump in 2016. Examining these processes from a discursive perspective highlights the conflictual negotiations through which members construct their understanding of reality and how political events are interpreted and charged with meaning. To do so, we draw on a body of literature within social movement theory that studies how political actors frame the meaning of events. This literature suggests that threats and opportunities pass through a process of social construction and attribution and must be constructed – framed – as collectively shared problems to have any impact on political mobilization. In this sense, the significance and meaning of events are not pre-determined; they are, in the words of the sociologist Robin Wagner-Pacifici (2017), "restless": they are contested sites of political semiosis, perpetual flows of meaning that rarely, if ever, crystallize.

What we find is what we refer to as "tribal epistemology". Unlike what the ideas of Habermas and the echo chamber thesis suggest, political communities do not arrive at their worldviews chiefly through the powers of rational deliberation and critical reasoning (Roberts, 2017). Instead, their view of the world is shaped by their particular interests and wishes, what they *want to be true*. Communities do not choose their positions based on rational evaluation of evidence, arguments, and counterarguments – but rather on whether the position supports the tribe's values and goals. Our reasoning and understanding of the world are inextricable from our identity and our community belonging.

Grassroots Framing

Collective action framing refers to the interpretative processes through which actors construct, maintain, and contest relevant meanings, beliefs and ideologies. These processes are not frictionless. They are contestable, negotiable, open to debate, and differential interpretation. There are often disagreements and internal conflicts between individuals and factions regarding how to interpret an issue or social problem and how to resolve it (Benford, 1993; Benford & Snow, 2000).

Such intramovement frame disputes typically concern different interpretations of reality – what is commonly referred to in the movement literature as
diagnostic frames. This includes defining some event or aspect of social life
as problematic, diagnosing the causes of the problem, and assigning blame.
But conflicts also derive from disparate visions on prognostic measures. Such
prognostic frames provide possible solutions to these problems and suggest
what must be done. This may include a plan of attack and suitable strategies
and tactics for carrying it out. In practice, there is often correspondence between diagnostic and prognostic frames since defining the problem and suggesting solutions are often parts of the same process. Together, these functions
provide a link between talk and action. While diagnostic frames foster and facilitate agreement, prognostic (and motivational) frames foster action, thereby
enabling activists to move from the balcony to the barricades (Benford &
Snow, 2000). The third important source of intramovement conflict concerns
which framing *strategy* is most effective. This does not concern what *is* or
ought to be real but how reality should be presented. What framing strategy
is most effective in order to get attention, attract sympathizers, and achieve
movement goals? This is conceptualized as *frame resonance*, and these strategic discussions often include tension or a difficult balance between ideological purity and opportunism.

Social movement scholars have commonly approached framing as a
strategic and top-down process orchestrated by movement leaders and organizations (Benford, 1997). As a result, empirical studies have typically
focused on how movement leaders present the movement to the public: how
they frame events to attract sympathizers, persuade the public, and motivate activists. This emphasis may reflect the difficulty of assessing internal
movement discussions, which can be challenging or even hazardous to obtain. Consequently, researchers have tended to analyze publicly available
sources, such as newsletters, flyers, and pronouncements by leaders and
protest organizers.

However, as Oliver and Johnston (2000) have observed, recasting the notion of collective action framing as solely an activity of movement leadership may obscure the interactive negotiations that occur among various actors
within the movement. The risk of treating framing as solely a top-down activity is it overlooks potential cleavages between different actors within the
movement. Consequently, what is studied may be a constructed image that
serves to legitimize the movement's political leaders rather than an accurate
representation of the lived experiences of the movement and its participants.
This may result in a distorted portrayal of the movement by its leaders.

Therefore, several scholars have called for more studies that focus on
the negotiations and conflictual processes that are intrinsic to the development of collective action frames (Castells, 2015; Earl, 2019; Schneider,
2005; Snow, Vliegenthart & Ketelaars, 2019). For instance, Benford
(1997, p. 422) advocates for the examination of "autonomous grassroots

movements as they first begin to organize mobilize around an issue", while Schneider (2005) argues for further study of intermediate processes that account for how shifts in opportunity factor into the strategic calculations of individuals and/or organizations.

Viewing framing as a process that takes place within digital spaces implies shifting the emphasis from leadership to grassroots members. Therefore, in this chapter, we focus on what we call *grassroots framing*. This refers to the bottom-up processes of meaning-making and collective negotiations that occur within movements in order to interpret and make sense of events. These processes are collective and emerge through interactions and movement discussions rather than being constructed by specific individuals or movement leaders.

Conventional frames, as typically presented by movement organizations, tend to be relatively consistent and integrated packages, polished to avoid contradictions and strategically designed to garner the support of politicians or to convince laypeople to become activists. In stark contrast, grassroots frames are not purposely designed for movement external purposes but are part of an ongoing process that occurs before frame crystallization. As such, grassroots frames are typically "frame embryos" or "half-cooked" frames that may contain fragments of diagnostic, prognostic, and motivational elements, but seldom all of them at the same time.

They tend to be fragmented and tentative, even contradictory and provocative. They are constructed in a process *by* and *for* movement actors rather than products that are designed specifically to be disseminated to the media and broader public. Social media and internet communities such as Stormfront function as arenas par excellence for these bottom-up processes of grassroots framing.

The Effect of Obama and Trump on Stormfront

The Obama 2008 election sparked a remarkable and unprecedented surge in the number of posts and newly registered users on Stormfront, illustrated in Figure 6.1. The number of first posts (the solid black line in the figure) and newly registered users (the dotted gray line) increased dramatically, with the day after the election seeing the highest number of new users in the history of the forum (2581 new users on November 5, 2008). Google Trends analytics also showed a significant increase in Google searches on "Stormfront forum" in November 2008, with most domestic searches originating from West Virginia, Arkansas, Oregon, and New Mexico, and most international searches originating from Serbia, Croatia, Great Britain, and Macedonia. In contrast, the re-election of Obama in 2012 and the election of Trump in 2016 had limited impact on user activity and posting activity, with new members and post numbers remaining relatively stable during these periods, as well as for all previous presidential elections since 2001.[2]

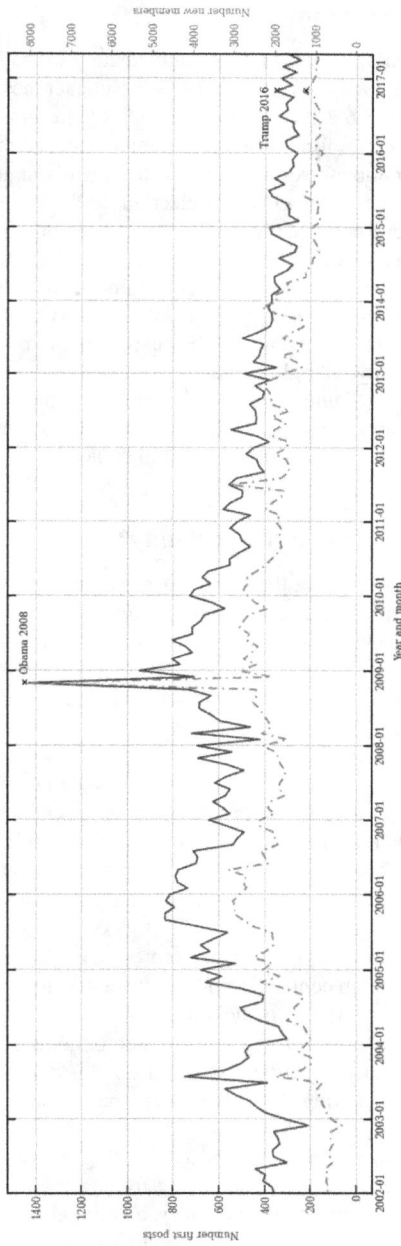

Figure 6.1 This figure shows the number of registered members per month (dotted gray line) alongside the number of members who made their first contribution to the forum each month (solid black line). It also highlights a significant discrepancy: while the total number of registered forum members is around 350,000, only about 100,000 of these have ever posted.

Discursive Work on Stormfront

Investigating the content of the posts in the immediate aftermath of the two elections provides us with a useful overview of what impact these events had on the community. Figure 6.2 depicts word clouds of the most distinctive emotional words on the entire forum for each Election Day and the day after,[3] thus highlighting the emotional words that most strongly distinguish one corpus compared to the other. After Obama's election 2008 (Figure 6.2a), the prevailing emotions were defeat and frustration, with common words such as "depressed", "disaster", "angry", "traitor", "scared", "protest", "puppet", and "trash". In contrast, Trump's election (Figure 6.2b) incited predominantly positive emotions, such as "happy", "promises", "victory", and "thanks". However, there were also emotional words that pointed in the opposite direction, such as "welcome", "right", and "good", for Obama and "worse", "sorry", and "destroy" for Trump, suggesting a more complex narrative. To explore this narrative further, we conducted a qualitative text analysis of the discussions, starting with the election of Obama in 2008.

Diagnosing Obama: Threat or Opportunity?

We analyzed all posts containing the word "Obama" over a two-week following the election. We selected this period because it contained the most relevant and topical discussions and made the corpus more manageable. This resulted in a subcorpus of 2,759 posts, which were chronologically ordered to facilitate temporal analyses. We used an inductive approach with open coding to analyze the posts, followed by a process of categorization and comparison of the established codes (Straus & Corbin, 1990). We then created a network visualization of the emerging codes using the Gephi software (see Figure 6.3). The nodes in the network represent what may call *frame components;* meaningful topics or arguments that explicitly relate to Obama. In line with previous discussions, these components can be understood as "frame embryos". They are fragments or pieces, rather than fully developed frames.

The edges between the nodes in the figure represent connections between two frame components. Such connection occurs when a single post contains more than one component. By using social network analysis, we generated a discursive network that illustrate how frame components are connected to each other, forming clusters. By analyzing these clusters, we may identify the underlying logic uniting them, which can be understood as a type of frame.

The results show two overarching and contrasting clusters of components that each represent a broader, underlying frame. The first cluster depicts President Obama as a threat to the country, a national disaster that will lead to chaos, whereas the second takes a different approach by framing the

(a)

(b)

Figure 6.2 This figure shows the most common emotional terms on the forum for the Election Day and the day after for, (a) Obama 2008, and (b) Trump, 2016. The words in the word clouds were calculated using Log-Likelihood comparisons between the word frequencies, using a list of emotional words. Accordingly, the word clouds illustrate the most distinctive emotional words for each respective time period. These calculations were conducted using the entire Stormfront corpus.

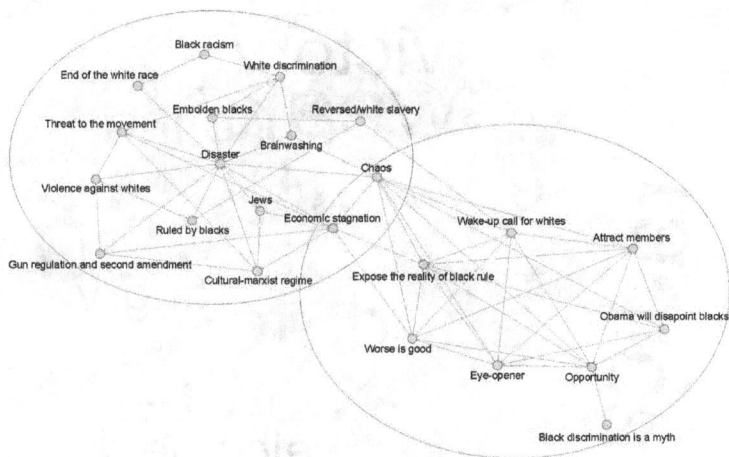

Figure 6.3 This figure shows a discursive network of frame components in posts within two weeks after Obama's election in 2008. The nodes represent frame components, and the ties represent overlaps of the frame components within posts.

election as a unique opportunity for the movement. The bolded words in the analysis below indicate that the word represents a node, or a frame component, in the network.

Obama as a Threat

Many members expressed frustration, desperation, and hopelessness, particularly in the first few days following the election. As one member concisely put it, "This country is finished. This empire, this civilization, this culture....I don't honestly believe there are nearly enough people who are, or ever will be willing to fight for its survival". This depiction of the Obama presidency as a threat is further elaborated in the following days and weeks. Many members argue that *chaos* will ensue as "negro rule" will drive American cities to become "crime-ridden, bankrupt slums". One member predicts "Black violence going totally unpunished, rampant miscegenation, and Whites being put into a subservient position. These things were already occurring before, but they will probably reach unprecedented levels". There is even a discussion thread for "doomsday prepping", consisting of a long list of various "necessary" items and preparations "in case of disaster", including food, water, and rifles.

The framing of President Obama as a threat is expressed in both racial and economic terms – both of which are dimensions of structural threats that tend to be prominent in social movement discourse (Almeida, 2019). In the former category are various posts describing the election as a victory for Blacks.

Obama's presidency is thus argued to further *embolden Blacks* and to contribute to spurring Black violence against Whites. As one member states:

> Power is slipping away more and more from good, honest, hardworking people. An undeclared war on Whites across the country has started. Negro pride is soaring, along with gay pride. It's only a matter of time before they start burning churches until the gov. gives in to their demands.

As evident in this post, there are also traces of a closely related and common frame component describing the election as a historical turning point, representing the start of *white slavery*. Word frequency analysis confirms that the terms "slave" and "slavery" spike during the day of the election (a 50% increase compared to the average during the two prior weeks), and indignant and ironic posts describe how Blacks once came as slaves, but have now progressed to having the most powerful position in the world: "You didn't hear? Whites are expected to report to the cotton fields at 8:00 sharp tomorrow morning". The fact that white men are now being ruled by a Black man awakened feelings of indignation and fury among these members: "For years, we've suffered the existence of Blacks, living among us as humans. Now, we'll suffer the indignity of being ruled by one of them; being ruled by an inferior being". Many members take this one step further, framing the election as the *end of the White race* – either through "race mixing" or through replacement and suppression/subjugation.

The framing of Obama as a threat is also expressed in economic terms, often as representing the establishment of a *Marxist-socialist regime.* Obama is thus alternately portrayed as a "Jewish socialist", a "liberal socialist Muslim", and perhaps most commonly, a "cultural Marxist". Along these lines, members describe how Obama's "Semitic communism" with "socialized medicine", "redistributed wealth", "taxation of the rich", and increased governmental regulation will lead to *economic stagnation.*

Obama as an Opportunity

As the immediate affections started to settle on the forum, a competing narrative emerged among the members, describing the election in more positive terms – as providing a **"window of opportunity"** or **"wake-up call"** for Whites. The notion of Obama as a threat is thus transformed and reconstructed as a unique opportunity for the movement to mobilize.

Activists promoting this narrative agreed that the Obama presidency will lead to *chaos* (as shown in Figure 6.3, this frame component links to both clusters), but frame this as an emerging opportunity for the movement.

> I think we should see this as more of an opportunity to change the world in which we live for the better. Maybe this is a new chance to recruit and spread our message faster and further than ever before. Remember, things will get much worse before they begin to get better and Obama might speed this process for us.

Some members even go as far as hoping for *more* radical liberal reforms and that Obama will be reelected for a second term:

> There will be a comeuppance and I am telling you that WORSE is better. Pray that it falls apart—so we can rebuild! May Obama rule the nation for 2 terms and not just 1! May Obama get every law passed that he wants to pass. May he get his way in EVERYTHING that he wants to do! Long live Obama!

The framing of Obama as an opportunity is manifested and expressed in various ways. One example is that it will reveal that ***Black discrimination is a myth*** and that the notion of White guilt is based on false premises.

> That argument is now null and void. A Black(half) man has proved that a Black(half) man can become President of the USA and now they can't blame 'Whitey' for everything that goes wrong in America in the next four years....I might like this Black President thing after all.

A closely related notion is that Obama's presidency will ***expose the consequences of the Black rule***. His failure will thus illustrate the "inferiority of the Black race". As one member puts it: "I'm not in the least bit angry that Obama was elected. I want to see him disappoint all of his believers and live up to everyone's worst fears. I don't want the happy illusion of a White President, I want the disastrous reality of Black rule and open racial conflict".

The underlying idea consolidating this cluster of frame components is that the threat of Obama will serve as a ***wake-up call*** or an ***eye-opener*** for White people, increasing racial awareness and contributing to racial polarization, thereby serving as a catalyst for radical change. This will, it is argued, ultimately serve to ***attract more people to the cause*** and to Stormfront. Along these lines, members frequently draw parallels to the *Turner Diaries*, a novel that describes how liberal and gun reforms sparked a resistance movement in the United States that eventually led to a violent revolution and race war.

> This may be a true wakeup call for the White race. White people who might have voted for a negro in the past, now are saying they WILL now vote along racial lines. The very fact that the Stormfront server was overwhelmed since the election bodes well for this movement. I've never seen it do that before!

The Final Solution: Plan of Attack

The election of Obama in 2008 also affected the prominent solutions – prognostic frames – promoted by activists on the forum. To study shifts in movement strategies following the election, we look specifically at posts containing "we should/must/need".[4]

We found two main categories of prognostic frames emerging after the election – both of which represent typical reactions to an imminent threat. Driven by hopelessness and frustration, one response is to ***emigrate***. As one member puts it: "Many of us believe there is no political solution to the question of White survival; therefore, leaving America is a logical option for young Whites". Another reaction is calling for the need to unite as a movement: to "keep strong", "not be discouraged", "stay together", "unite as a people", "get organized", and "don't give up". "Our race is dying by the day. It's not the time to play stupid games. We need each other now more than ever, and we need to put petty differences aside". Many activists also encourage each other to brace for increasing political repression and "prepare for that pro-Caucasian sites like this might be shut down". Some members even call for arming themselves and to "get your gun out of storage".

However, as the Obama presidency becomes reframed as an opportunity rather than a threat, the focus shifts to emphasizing the need to adapt movement strategies to make the best of the situation. Consequently, we may discern an emerging theme composed of more reflexive and self-critical posts calling to reconsider established strategies and methods within the movement. As one member expresses: "We need to get organized because we cannot just react to situations. We need to organize, plan, act and react. We need to lead or race to the forefront and get back what is ours". Looking at the long-term discussions during the three months after the election, two main conflicting frames emerge concerning how the movement should reassess its political strategies during the Obama presidency: either to *fight against the system* or to *fight within the system*.

Fight the System

This frame conveys widespread skepticism regarding the idea of achieving radical change within the established political system. As one member succinctly puts it: "We cannot win by the ballot box". Some members have completely given up hope in the established political system after Obama's victory and instead advocate more dramatic changes in terms of "turning the system on its head": "We need a war, and we need it NOW". While a political revolution is indeed an end goal many members on the forum subscribe to, there is broad consensus on the forum that this is not realistic for the time being.

A more common strategy, therefore, is to advocate for the creation of autonomous communities, i.e., some kind of free spaces that "depart from old social rules" and prefigure the types of structures they wish to see. In other words, "a model community", or a "Stormfront of the streets". This is often discussed in terms of creating autonomous geographical territories by buying up land. Some activists advocate the creation of cultural or discursive spaces (e.g., book clubs and white schools). These types of free spaces are portrayed as vital not only to preserve and develop their own culture and racial identity but also to spread their values outside of these protected communities and attract the support of, for example, former Republican white voters. This recalls how the social movement literature often emphasizes the role of "free social spaces" and "cultural havens" in fostering the development of collective identity and oppositional culture in progressive movements (e.g., Evans, 1979; Fraser, 1990).

Fight Within the System

The second main prognostic frame takes a radically different approach, advocating instead to fight within the system. This idea often co-occurs with the diagnostic frame that presents Obama as a wake-up call that will radicalize the Republican grassroots and enforce White identity within the Republican Party. "The atmosphere in the grassroots is getting to a point where our people are choking and gasping for fresh air. Time to present it". In a much-discussed post on the forum, former KKK leader David Duke presents two alternative political routes within this frame that came to define the subsequent discussions: "We will either take the Republican Party back over the next four years or we will say, 'To Hell With the Republican Party!' And we will take 90 percent of Republicans with us into a New Party that will take its current place!" This issue divides many members and sparks intense debate regarding whether to create a new White nationalist party or rebuild the Republican party and radicalize it from below.

Along these lines, there is a broadly shared realization among many members that, to "attract average White folks" and channel existing public discontent against Obama into the movement, they must polish their public image. This represents a type of *frame alignment* in the sense that activists argue for changing their appearance in accordance with the mainstream, play down the most radical aspects of their ideology, and avoid explicit references to Stormfront and other racist organizations, a process that resembles the strategy used by the KKK in the 1970–1980s: "We need to make WNs [White nationalists] respectable and attractive to the moderate middle-class White America, we need to wear coats and ties instead of military uniforms".

To sum up thus far, the analysis has revealed a tension between two contrasting diagnostic frames on how to interpret and make sense of the election of Obama in 2008, each based on a converse logic that can be expressed as "worse is worse" versus "worse is better". These are, in turn, connected with two corresponding prognostic frames advocating to either "fight within the system" or "fight outside or against the system". As we will see in the next section, these frames reappear in discussions after the election of Trump in 2016, although an interesting shift occurs.

Diagnosing Trump: Can He Be Trusted?

While Obama was, at least initially, framed as a threat creating a sense of urgency and outrage among white supremacists, the election of Trump in 2016 was initially framed as an opening in the political-institutional system.

Although this election did not have any significant effects in terms of member activity, it is clear that optimism and anticipation prevailed during the first few days after the election. In this step, we used the same methodological approach as when analyzing the Obama corpus, but this time, we look at all posts containing the term "Trump" over a two-week period following Election Day, resulting in a subcorpus of 2,186 posts.

Looking closer at the discussions during the first few days, there is an abundance of *triumphant and celebratory* posts framing the election as an important victory for the white race and white nationalist movement. These posts are combined with malicious comments about *snowflakes and crying liberals* and ironic calls to the celebrities who took a public stance against Trump to do as promised and emigrate from the United States. In the discussions during the two weeks to come, we may discern three prominent approaches to Trump on the forum (see Figure 6.4). While the first two are mainly positive, framing the election as a "turnaround" or at least as a "step in the right direction", the third takes a more critical stance.

Trump Presidency as a Great Victory

In the more optimistic camp, Trump's presidency is framed as a *great opportunity* and turnaround for the movement: "It will be a major deterrent and a symbol that they are not as welcome as they thought they once were.

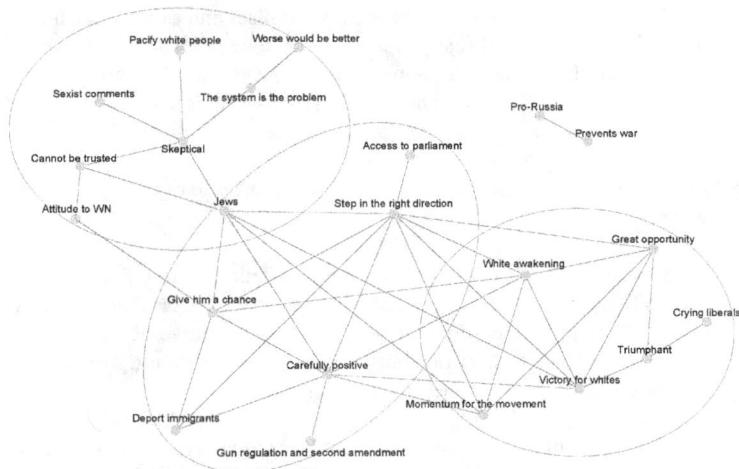

Figure 6.4 This figure shows a network of frame components in posts within two weeks after trump's election in 2016. The subcorpus comprises all posts containing the term "Trump" over a two-week period following the election (n: 2,186 posts).

The illegals will roam the streets and be reported and arrested. The wall will inspire patriotism in several Whites. This election has been a turnaround for us". There is a broadly shared belief that the Trump presidency will lead to radical and large-scale changes regarding a range of issues like immigration policies, taxes, gun regulation, and education.

Similar to the election of Obama in 2008, the Trump presidency is framed in racial terms, but this time as a *victory for whites*. "TRUMP WON! Just goes to show you that when the White Working Class turns out to vote, they can still swing an election!" While Obama was argued to incite racial awareness among Whites, the election of Trump is thus framed as the result of such a *white awakening*. In other words, according to this narrative, white people were empowered by Obama but emboldened by Trump. As one member expressed it, Trump is seen as "essentially the voice of disempowered, disenfranchised, displaced, ignored White Americans who are rapidly losing the civilization and nation White Americans created".

A Step in the Right Direction

A second cluster of frame components expresses slightly more cautious and guarded – but nonetheless *carefully positive* – attitudes. While Trump is not seen as "one of us", he nonetheless represents a "tiny ray of light in the filthy blackness of liberalism". This is expressed in various calls to "bide our time and sit tight" and to "see what he does". This is often accompanied by doubts about whether he will actually deliver on his promises and calls for the movement to remain vigilant. "I really want to believe he is legit. To believe the rare off chance that he isn't a puppet is hard, but it would be great. We as citizens must remain vigilant". Thus, while Trump is not seen as a permanent solution or as representing any dramatic change, he is nonetheless framed as one **small** *step in the right direction.* By providing the movement some respite, he offers "breathing room" that makes it easier to organize and show what is possible.

> We all went into this election knowing that Trump is not, nor ever will be a WN let alone the 21st century Hitler. Trump is far from what the ideal WN candidate could ever be.... But I do believe he can accomplish most of what we want, but it will be very difficult. We have to wait and see.

With this reasoning, many activists emphasize that Trump will, at minimum, pursue a number of practical policy actions in line with the interests of the movement, such as *deporting immigrants* and thwarting any attempts of *gun regulation.* While he may not be seen as the answer to all problems, "he is at least better than the alternative". As one member aptly expresses, "I say support him but keep your guns loaded".

Trump Cannot Be Trusted

A third cluster expresses more critical attitudes toward the Trump presidency, claiming that the election constitutes a "double-edged sword" that risks contributing to *pacifying White people*. Interestingly, this represents a return of the "worse is better" narrative in the claim that the *system is the problem*, and therefore, the Trump presidency is, at best, a "bump in the road" or, at worst, "part of the cancer, but more subtle". As one member expressed:

> I don't put much stock on Trump delivering all his promises. The $ystem itself is the problem. It has to go, and be rebuilt from the ground up to suit the needs of the White majority not Jewish [*sic*] globalist political crime syndicates.... I've always said that we aren't going to win this thing by voting.

Following this reasoning, some members call for others to stop supporting Trump or encouraging people from believing that the system can be reformed from within. In this sense, Trump is framed as a larger threat than Obama since he is merely a "mediocre civic nationalist who will plunge in deeper sleep our awakening siblings!" What is needed is, as one member claims: "extreme polarization in every aspect of our lives to awaken the majority of the White people".

Overall, the discussions that take place during the two weeks after the election can be described as a struggle between positive and skeptical members. As illustrated in the overlap of frame components in Figure 6.4, there are two main reasons for this division. The first concerns Trump's alleged connections to *Jews*, where critical members frame him as a Jewish puppet based on his positive stance toward Israel, having selected Jews for central positions in the administration, and having Jews in his family. While acknowledging this, more positive members accentuate that it "could be worse", and that "he is at least independent". A second source of conflict concerns Trump's public *attitudes toward white nationalists*. The discussions go back and forth between those arguing that since he is not a white nationalist, he "cannot be trusted", and others defending his position by arguing that public support for white nationalists would be political suicide.

Altogether, the friction between the "worse is better" and "better is better" frames is still prominent on the forum after Trump, but the latter frame seems to have now gained traction. By framing Trump as an opportunity that provides momentum for the movement, both positive and more cautious members adhere to this underlying frame. Accordingly, the "worse is better" frame that dominated the discussions after Obama is now less common, and in fact, many activists now appear explicitly critical of this strategy, pointing to its potential risks:

> America has no nationalist party and has a rapidly increasing non-White population. I don't think there's enough time to employ the 'worse is better' strategy there. As such I can't see the harm Trump being elected can really bring in this situation.

Shifting Strategies: Toward Institutionalization

As the "better is better" frame dominates the discourse after Trump, members also tend to be more positive toward the idea of achieving change through the means of the political system. When looking closer at posts containing "we should/must/need",[5] there is a broadly shared view among the members that Trump's presidency has served to legitimize the movement and open (discursive) space within the established political system to air ideas that were previously banned and stigmatized: "We should be peaceful and solve our problems through the 'system', abiding by all the laws, and setting examples such that we become role models for everyone to emulate". Thus, as the crisis in political representation settles, the idea of creating a third political party also wanes.

The election of Trump has legitimized many of our ideas and thoughts within the Republican Party. It is now possible for WN's pro-Whites to express themselves politically under the umbrella of the Republican Party without being automatically tarred as an outsider/nut. Just be smart and careful with the language you use. The name of the game is power and now is the perfect time to get involved in the political struggle for the future of Whites in the United States.

This shift in outgroup construction on the community and a decreasing skepticism toward the government and established political institutions after Trump can also be observed in a word embedding analysis of the community.[6] This analysis looks at words that were most closely associated with words indicating an out-group (e.g., "they", "them", "those"). As shown in Figure 6.5, "Blacks", "minorities", and "Jews", are consistently the most frequently recurring oppositional categories on the forum. "Illegals" and "invaders" became more central as an out-group following the election of Trump, while the use of "homosexuals", "females", and "women" decreased. One possible explanation is that women were largely blamed for voting for Obama. But the most striking result is that the use of terms such as "government", "ZOG" ("Zionist occupation government"), and "police" decreased in significance as out-groups after the election of Trump, indicating that members may have become less skeptical toward the government and established political institutions.

Both the quantitative and qualitative analysis thus suggest that members of the forum now seem increasingly geared toward institutionalization, and the idea of achieving change outside the system is now less often expressed. As part of this trend toward institutionalization, the main task and role of the movement thus appears to shift, as Trump is seen as an entrance to political power. The general political strategy now is to, as one member expressed it: "connect ourselves to as many centers of power as possible while excluding our enemies from those same centers". This is also evident in that activists start to reformulate the goals of the movements, increasingly defining their role and function in relation to the government – their tasks are to "influence

The 'Other' after elections of Obama and Trump

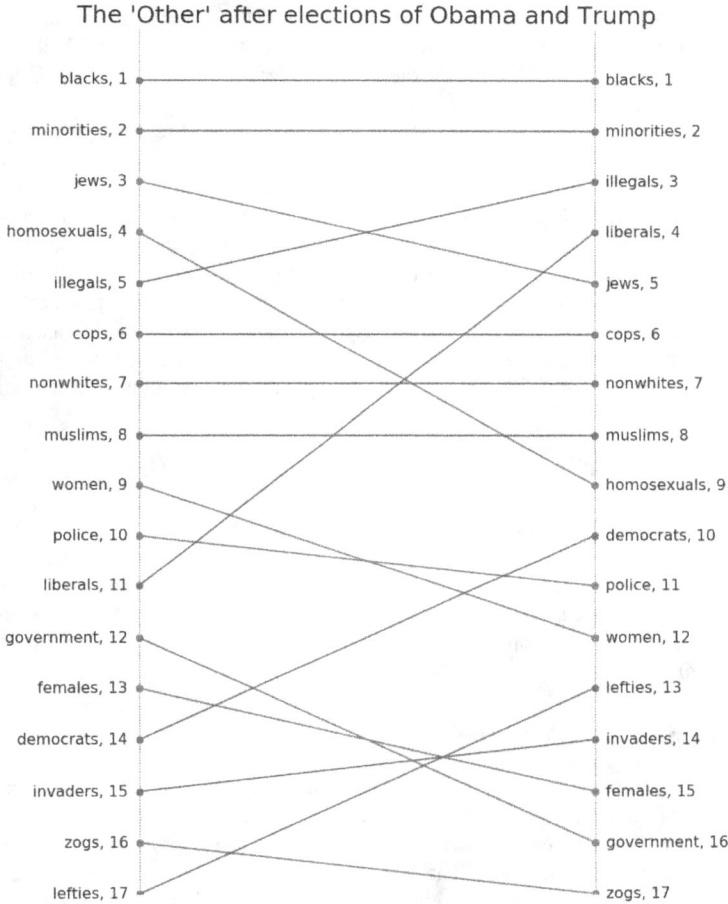

blacks, 1 — blacks, 1
minorities, 2 — minorities, 2
jews, 3 — illegals, 3
homosexuals, 4 — liberals, 4
illegals, 5 — jews, 5
cops, 6 — cops, 6
nonwhites, 7 — nonwhites, 7
muslims, 8 — muslims, 8
women, 9 — homosexuals, 9
police, 10 — democrats, 10
liberals, 11 — police, 11
government, 12 — women, 12
females, 13 — lefties, 13
democrats, 14 — invaders, 14
invaders, 15 — females, 15
zogs, 16 — government, 16
lefties, 17 — zogs, 17

Figure 6.5 "The other". Word embedding analysis of outgroups. This figure shows shifts in outgroups in the community in a 6-month period after each election day. As the graph shows, "Blacks" remains the main outgroup in the community after both elections. "Liberals", "illegals", "democrats", and "lefties" increased somewhat in relevance after Trump, while words related to political institutions ("police", "government", and "zog") decreased after Trump.

Trump", to "push him to the right", and – commonly – to be "fire to his feet". Interestingly, these comments are often interwoven with an implicit or explicit skepticism against Trump, claiming that "he cannot be fully trusted" and that "he is not one of us". Therefore, the movement must remain "constantly vigilant" and "make sure he delivers". For instance, as two members express:

"We must make certain he carries out his two MOST important campaign promises. Build The Wall and round up millions of illegals. Otherwise all hell will break loose", and "We must keep Trump's feet to the fire. When not if but when he turns on us. We must be ready".

By embedding a system-positive approach in critical terms in this way, it can be interpreted as a type of counterframing – a way of neutralizing the arguments from the "worse is better" frame regarding the potential risks associated with institutionalization. A related and common strategy is to accentuate the agency of the movement. In other words, the opportunity provided by Trump lies not in the fact that he himself will contribute to radical change but rather that he will contribute by creating a space for the movement to mobilize and pursue its own agenda. Accordingly, there are frequent calls to "use the momentum", "step up", "take a leading role", and "not trust that the government will do it for us". As one user vividly expresses this in the aftermath of the election:

> My dear fellow Stormfront members, Trump won, now what? Do we go back to sleep as we did during the Reagan years allowing him to give amnesty to 3 million illegal invaders? ... No! Do we take a back seat and reach out an olive branch to the traitorous cucks who have worked to destroy our country and our very existence? No! The time to be aggressive and proactive is NOW. We may never have another chance like this in our lifetimes! This is only the beginning of a new bright and glorious future for our people!

Conclusion

This chapter has revealed the collective negotiations around competing versions of reality that take place on Stormfront, a process we term grassroots framing. This concept describes the bottom-up processes through which movement actors themselves attempt to make sense of dramatic events and unravel their implications for the movement. We found that the discursive creation of opportunity was a consistent key driver of the framing process aimed at identifying an optimistic interpretation. The framings that gained traction in the discussions were those that constituted effective responses to questions such as, "How can we frame this event as positive and empowering for our movement?" and "What openings for political action can we find here?" This provides empirical support for Gamson and Meyer's (1996) observation that activists tend to favor frames that create a role for the movement and opportunities for action.

Movement actors thus bend, reformulate, recontextualize, and narrativize events to make them appear beneficial for the movement's opportunities; they try to create ways forward. For example, members of Stormfront initially described the election of Obama as a disaster, but over time, they increasingly converted to a framing that transformed this disaster into a great opportunity that could increase race awareness, attract activists, and serve as a wake-up call for white Americans. This illustrates a "worse is better" diagnostic framing.

Conversely, the election of Trump in 2016 was described as a good thing for the movement by bringing hope, increasing momentum, and showing what is possible. Accordingly, the "worse is better" frame was increasingly replaced by a "better is better" frame. In a similar vein, the election led to a shift in political strategies: from advocating the extraparliamentary methods that dominated after Obama to an increasing belief in the possibilities of achieving radical change through the established political system. This means that what is sometimes presented as a contradiction in the literature on political opportunities is, in fact, coherent: *both* openings and closures of political opportunities can be empowering to movements, given that the movements invest the necessary discursive labor. When *bad is good*, and *good is good*, everything can become empowering.

This analysis highlights that online communities like Stormfront may provide a space where users collectively create interpretations of reality that guide their understanding of problems and potential solutions. Narrative construction is an evolving and emergent process, an interpretive action, that comes into being when persons, along with others, attempt to make sense of self and world. Rather than harmonious and consensual, this takes place through a dialectical process fraught with conflict, hazards, and fragility, as different movement actors are fighting it out over how to frame and understand the opportunities and challenges of a changing reality. Narratives provide comfort and a sense of security; they give guidance for how we can understand reality, ourselves, and our roles in it. By participating in the processes of co-creating these narratives, we simultaneously become part of the community. In this way, the formation of narratives is intertwined with identity construction.

While the Habermasian story suggested that political communities arrive at their position through rational deliberation – if at times founded on faulty grounds – we have here outlined a Durkheimian perspective on community reasoning. We found what can be described as a form of "tribal epistemology", in which stories are evaluated not on common standards of evidence but on whether they support our tribe's values and goals. What is "good for our side" and "true" becomes nearly impossible to distinguish.

The Durkheimian perspective thus offers an explanation of the observed link between echo chambers and the rise of misinformation. As communities form within these spaces, they build their own worldviews based on what they wish to be true. These spaces thus give room for the growth of conspiracies that are disconnected from reality, as the members so strongly *want* something to be true to keep their connection with their community. Truth becomes a question of identity, as information is evaluated based not on common standards of evidence applied to commonly accepted facts but on its alignment with our social identity. Our very ways of knowing become defined by identity and belonging, and what we know is reduced to just another expression of who we are.

Notes

1 An earlier version of this chapter was published as "'Wake-up call for the white race': How Stormfront framed the elections of Obama and Trump", in *Mobilization: An International Quarterly, 26*(3), 285–302. Reprinted by permission of Mobilization.

2 Another event that generated much traffic to the website was the terrorist attack in Norway in 2008. In 24 hours after the killings, 4,481 members were online, a record that stands to this day. Alexa, which monitors Web traffic, shows that Stormfront visits spiked globally on the day of the Oslo attacks.

3 The words in the word clouds were calculated using log-likelihood comparisons between the word frequencies, using a pre-set list of emotional words. Accordingly, the word clouds illustrate the most distinctive emotional words for each time period. These calculations were run on all posts during each Election day and the day after.

4 To analyze prognostic frames, we created a new subcorpus by selecting all posts within the previous subcorpus containing "we should/must/need". We then divided this subcorpus into two periods: (1) within three days after the election (Obama: 126 posts), (2) within three months (Obama: 669 posts). This provides us with a more dynamic account of framing, enabling us to capture both immediate reactions but also more strategic reflections developing over time.

5 To analyze prognostic frames after Trump, we used the same approach as for Obama. We included all posts in this subcorpus containing "we should/must/need" and divided this into two periods: (1) within three days after the election (Trump: 135 posts), (2) within three months (Obama: 769 posts).

6 Word embedding analysis (or word2vec) is a set of language modeling techniques where words are mapped to vectors of real numbers in such a way that words with similar meanings have a similar representation (Goldberg and Levy 2014). In other words, it aims to quantify and categorize semantic similarities between linguistic items based on their distributional properties in large samples of language data. To analyze the conception of "them" in these materials, the word-embedding space was projected on a line spanned between the average of a selection of words associated with "us" ("we", "us", "our", "ours", "ourself", "ourselves", "ally", "allies", "hero", "heroes") and "them" ("they", "them", "their", "theirs", "themselves"). This essentially positions words on a line between "us" and "them", thereby revealing who is conceived of as the in-group and out-group, respectively. The first 200 words most closely associated with "them" were manually filtered for nouns describing groups. The corpus comprises all posts within 6 months after each election.

References

Almeida, P. D. (2019). The role of threat in collective action. In D. A. Snow, S. A. Soule, & H. Kriesi (Eds.), *Wiley-Blackwell companion to social movements* (pp. 43–62). Oxford: Blackwell.

Benford, R. D. (1993). Frame disputes within the nuclear disarmament movement. *Social forces, 71*(3), 677–701.

Benford, R. D. (1997). An insider's critique of the social movement framing perspective. *Sociological inquiry, 67*(4), 409–430.

Benford, R. D., & Snow, D. A. (2000). Framing processes and social movements: An overview and assessment. *Annual reviews*, 26(1), 611–639.

Castells, M. (2015). *Networks of outrage and hope: Social movements in the internet age*. London: John Wiley & Sons.

Earl, J. (2019). Technology and social media. In D. Snow, S. Soule, H. Kriesi, & H. McCammon (Eds.), *The Wiley Blackwell companion to social movements* (pp. 289)). Oxford: John Wiley & Sons Ltd.

Evans, S. M. (1979). *Personal politics: The roots of women's liberation in the civil rights movement and the new left* (Vol. 228). London: Vintage.

Fraser, N. (1990). Rethinking the public sphere: A contribution to the critique of actually existing democracy. *Social text*, (25/26), 56–80.

Gamson, W. A., & Meyer, D. S. (1996). Framing political opportunity. In D. McAdam, J. D. McCarthy, & M. N. Zald (Eds.), *Comparative perspectives in social movements: Political opportunities, mobilizing structures and cultural framing* (pp. 275–290). Cambridge: Cambridge University Press.

Goldberg, Y., & Levy, O. (2014). word2vec Explained: Deriving Mikolov et al.'s negative-sampling word-embedding method. *arXiv preprint arXiv:1402.3722*.

Howell, L. (2013). Digital wildfires in a hyperconnected world. *WEF report*, *3*, 15–94.

Oliver, P. E., & Johnston, H. (2000). What a good idea: Frames and ideologies in social movements research. *Mobilization: An international journal*, 5(1), 37–54.

Poushter, J., Fagan, M., & Gubbala, S. (2022). Climate Change Remains Top Global Threat Across 19-Country Survey. *Pew Research Center's Global Attitudes Project*. https://www.pewresearch.org/global/2022/08/31/climate-change-remains-top-global-threat-across-19-country-survey/

Roberts, D. (2017). *Donald Trump and the rise of tribal epistemology*. Vox Media. https://www.vox.com/policy-and-politics/2017/3/22/14762030/donald-trump-tribal-epistemology

Schneider, C. (2005). Almeida. In H. Johnston & J. A. Noakes (Eds.), *Frames of protest: Social movements the framing perspective* (pp. 163–181). Oxford: Rowman & Littlefield.

Snow, D. A., Vliegenthart, R., & Ketelaars, P. (2019). The framing perspective on social movements: Its conceptual roots and architecture. In D. Snow, S. Soule, H. Kriesi, & H. McCammon (Eds.), *The Wiley Blackwell companion to social movements* (pp. 392–410). Oxford: Wiley Blackwell.

Straus, A., & Corbin, J. (1990). *Basics of qualitative research: Grounded theory procedures and techniques*. Newbury Park, CA: Sage.

Törnberg, P. (2018). Echo chambers and viral misinformation: Modeling fake news as complex contagion. *PloS one*, 13(9), e0203958.

Vosoughi, S., Roy, D., & Aral, S. (2018). The spread of true and false news online. *Science*, 359(6380), 1146–1151.

Wagner-Pacifici, R. (2017). *What is an event?* Chicago: University of Chicago Press.

7 Affect

Building Emotional Energy

Emotions are at the core of Durkheim's rituals. In the previous chapter, we examined how Stormfront facilitates the construction of a shared worldview among members of the platform. As we observed, this process is not solely a matter of language and stories; it involves deeply emotional experiences, as our narratives are produced through a social process that is inextricably intertwined with our identity and self-understanding. Consequently, our stories are not merely narrated but are viscerally *felt*.

Our narratives situate us within our community, providing a sense of security and comfort. When they are challenged – either by arguments or events incongruent with our understanding of the world – our connections to our social context are threatened, resulting in strong emotional reactions. As we have seen, communities can offer ways to reject such threats by simply disregarding evidence and creating their own versions of events. The outcome is the creation of stories that may have little connection to reality.

However, for individuals not shielded by the protective tribal epistemology of a community, threatening events that challenge their stories can undermine the very foundation of their self-understanding. These types of personal crises are referred to in social movement literature as "moral shocks" (Jasper, 1998), "suddenly imposed grievance" (McAdam, 1982), or "quotidian disruptions" (Snow et al., 1998). They can lead to strong reactions, as they challenge a group's values and interests, disrupt their self-image and identity, and result in feelings of outrage, indignation, fear, or disgust (Snow & Soule, 2010; Warren, 2010). This chapter focuses on an event that was deeply traumatic for many white supremacists in the United States: the 2008 election of Obama.

For most Americans, Barack Obama's 2008 election represented the proud culmination of decades of historical progress, marking the election of an individual who, only a generation earlier, would have been barred from entering a movie theatre in parts of the country. But for others, the election was experienced as deeply unsettling – a threat to something unspoken at the very core of their understanding of themselves as white Americans. For these individuals, the event was less comprehended than it was *felt* – an uprooting of their sense of the *natural order of things*. The election of a Black man – articulate,

DOI: 10.4324/9781003108344-8

well-educated, intelligent – as president meant that the presumed superiority upon which their white identity had implicitly rested, without their awareness or admission, was now called into question. This event, therefore, provides a suitable case for investigating how traumas affect online communities and how these events are collectively negotiated and transformed.

On Stormfront, the election of Obama drove an unprecedented inflow of new users, who experienced the event as deeply distressing and sought a community through which to process it. This chapter uses our Durkheimian framework to examine how Stormfront provides a space for creating and disseminating narratives that imbue meaning to feelings of anxiety and despair, as well as the social processes involved in constructing those narratives. As we saw in Chapter 2, the rituals taking place in online communities centrally operate in the realm of emotions. These processes can help to transform passive feelings into emotional energy and a sense of collective identity, which, in turn, drives movement action. Focusing on this aspect also provides insight into how forums like Stormfront fulfill emotional functions for movements: they provide a space for emotional transformation. In this context, we argue that Stormfront functioned as a type of "digital therapy group" or an "emotional refuge" (Reddy, 2001) for white supremacists. We will draw on the concept of "cultural trauma", to examine why individuals join extremist online communities.

Cultural Trauma

Emile Durkheim described how collective trauma arises from a social crisis that threatens a community's way of life, leading to feelings of helplessness, moral confusion, and a sense of loss (Durkheim, 1912). For Durkheim, this concept primarily emphasizes the impact of traumatic events on the social integration and moral fabric of a society, causing disruptions to its social order and collective consciousness. Jeffrey Alexander's (2004) concept of *cultural trauma* builds upon Durkheim's ideas but places a greater emphasis on the role of narrative construction and symbolic representations in shaping collective memory and understanding of traumatic events. Cultural trauma theory holds that certain events have indelible and enduring effects on collective identity, as they represent an "acute discomfort entering into the core of the collectivity's sense of its own identity" (Alexander, 2004, p. 10). Alexander describes cultural trauma as a social process involving the disruption of the cultural basis of social order, eliciting emotions such as anxiety, fear, distrust, pessimism, and insecurity (see also Eyerman, 2004, 2022; Sztompka, 2004).

The notion of cultural trauma is fundamentally different from psychoanalytic notions of trauma (Caruth, 2016; LaCapra, 2014): unlike psychological trauma, cultural trauma is created through the "symbolic extension" of victimhood from the individual to the collective level. It is primarily experienced through various mediated forms, including narratives, testimonials, and witness accounts, propaganda, and news coverage. Cultural trauma theory thus opposes naturalist theories that understand trauma as inherently associated with large-scale events, such as war and atrocities, by instead arguing that cultural traumas are "made, not born" (Smelser, 2004, p. 37).

While characterizing the election of the first Black president in the United States as traumatic for white supremacists may appear hyperbolic or even provocative, its technical meaning does not imply any objective severity of the event itself but includes any events that challenge the self-narrative and identity of a community. In this context, we argue that the election posed a challenge to the core self-understanding of certain whites as belonging to a "superior race", by questioning foundational narratives of identity that are ubiquitous in the United States, with deep roots in the historical context of slavery and Jim Crow segregation.

Alexander's conceptualization highlights the importance of various organized actors and institutions, such as the media, political leaders, and intellectuals, in interpreting and attributing meaning to traumatic events. Such *trauma narratives* offer meaning and coherence to feelings of pain, suffering, and confusion. These narratives tell a story of what happened to "us", who is culpable, and what should be done to repair "our" collectivity. For Durkheim, religious beliefs and practices fulfilled this function: to make sense of traumas, help people understand the cause of their suffering, and find a way forward. Religious beliefs thus provide a sense of order and stability in times of crisis, reinforcing social norms and creating a sense of shared identity. As Alexander posits, there may be several competing narratives, each representing different visions for resolving the tensions. Sociologist Philip Smith (2010, p. 18) defines trauma narratives similarly:

> Narratives allocate causal responsibility for action, define actors and give them motivation, indicate the trajectory of past episodes and predict consequences of future choices, suggest courses of action, confer and withdraw legitimacy, and provide social approval by aligning events with normative cultural codes. Social action can be seen as deeply embedded in a narrative framework. People make sense of the world with stories and act accordingly.

By providing a framework of meaning that helps people make sense of the world, trauma narratives thus weave individual experiences of fear, anger, and suffering into collective stories aimed at repairing a collective identity. As we will demonstrate in this chapter, the construction and dissemination of trauma narratives are not necessarily performed by organized groups and movement intellectuals, as suggested by Alexander, but can also occur in a more decentralized manner through the collective negotiations between users on online platforms. In these cases, we argue, the social and interactive process of formulating a trauma narrative, in which people come together to share their emotions and experiences, can itself be a powerful tool for healing and strengthening collective identity and in-group solidarity.

Building on Durkheim, Collins (2004, 2009) emphasizes that during times of crisis and trauma, people tend to come together and synchronize their thoughts and actions, finding support and comfort in the community. Traumatic experiences thus tend to elicit collective manifestations or community rituals, manifesting through demonstrations and other forms of collective action, as well as through interpersonal communication (although this has been less studied). As Collins argues, participating in these types of collective manifestations, or interaction rituals, may serve to transform traumas into emotional energy and group solidarity, as the "ritualized sharing of instigating or initiating emotions which brought individuals to the collective gathering in the first place (outrage, anger, fear, etc.) gives rise to distinctively collective emotions, the feelings of solidarity, enthusiasm, and morality" (Collins, 2009, p. 29). Participants in (successful) interaction rituals thus develop a mutual focus of attention and become animated by each other's micro-rhythms and emotions. According to Collins, the results of these interaction chains are group solidarity, emotional energy (feelings of confidence, elation, strength, enthusiasm, initiative for action), symbols that represent the group, and feelings of morality.

As we saw in Chapter 2, key components in a successful online interaction ritual are shared emotional mood, barriers to outsiders, and mutual focus of attention. We here focus in particular on the emotional dimensions of the ritual: the importance of perceived emotional synchrony for successful rituals, and their emotional consequences. In an interaction ritual, participants generate emotional energy through the mutual reinforcement of their shared emotions, leading to a sense of solidarity and attachment to the group. To elaborate on the interplay between emotional exchanges, group cohesion, and collective identity, we find Jasper's distinction between different types of emotions in social interaction particularly useful.

Jasper (2008) distinguishes between *reciprocal emotions* and *shared emotions*. He defines reciprocal emotions as the emotions individuals experience in response to the emotions of others within a group or social context. These emotions potentially bolster social bonds and facilitate cooperation among group members by fostering a sense of empathy and understanding. For instance, when one person expresses anger or sadness about an issue, others may reciprocate these emotions, leading to a shared emotional experience that can strengthen group cohesion and propel collective action. These emotions comprise what Goodwin (1997) has referred to as the "libidinal economy" of a movement, yielding many of the pleasures of protest.

In contrast, *shared emotions* refer to the collective emotional experiences that arise from a common cause or event, such as a shared trauma or victory. These emotions reflect how the group collectively nurtures anger towards outsiders, such as outrage over government policies. They can foster unity and solidarity among group members, reinforcing their collective identity and commitment to a common goal. Shared emotions can also serve as a powerful motivator for collective action, as individuals are driven by their emotional connection to the cause and their fellow group members. Jasper argues that the power of shared emotions derives from their collective expression, with shared and reciprocal emotions reinforcing each other and enhancing solidarity within a movement or community. He states:

> Each measure of shared outrage against a nuclear plant reinforces the reciprocal emotion of fondness for others precisely because they feel the same way. They are like us; they understand. Conversely mutual affection is one context in which new shared emotions are easily created. Because you are fond of others, you want to adopt their feelings.
>
> (Jasper, 2008, p. 187)

Both Jasper's notions of reciprocal and shared emotions, as well as Collins' concept of interaction rituals emphasize the importance of emotional exchanges in shaping social interactions and collective action. In this light, reciprocal emotions can be seen as a driving force behind the formation and perpetuation of interaction ritual chains. As individuals engage in social encounters and exchange emotional cues, they generate and maintain reciprocal emotions, which contribute to the emotional energy that sustains the interaction ritual chain. Meanwhile, shared emotions can be understood as an outcome of successful interaction rituals. When participants in an interaction ritual achieve a shared emotional mood, they experience shared emotions that fortify group cohesion and solidarity. This sense of unity and belonging, in turn, encourages continued participation in interaction ritual chains and reinforces collective identity.

To summarize thus far, we propose that the construction of trauma narratives should be approached as a *social process*. Both the trauma narratives themselves and the participation in the collective processes (or interaction rituals) that generate them potentially impart meaning and coherence to feelings of pain, fear, and confusion. It is, therefore, reasonable to infer that potentially traumatic events could impact different groups or individuals within a movement or community differently, and similarly that the mechanisms by which these traumas are addressed could vary. Individuals or groups with access to pre-developed narratives and a strong sense of community support may be better equipped to cope with crisis and trauma. In contrast, those who lack these resources may react differently. In the subsequent sections, we will empirically investigate these processes by comparing long-term users with new users on Stormfront.

The Obama Effect on Stormfront

As we have seen in the previous chapter, the election of the first black president in the United States was a seismic event on the forum, sparking all-time-high recruitment to the website. The number of first posts skyrocketed, and the number of newly registered members in the days surrounding the election was by far the highest in the history of the forum. The event also triggered intense emotional reactions, with many members expressing feelings of defeat and frustration in the immediate aftermath of the election. However, while the 2008 election had a profound impact on online activity on Stormfront, not all user groups responded in the same way. As we will explore in this chapter, the increased activity in the community was driven by specific user groups, and, even more interestingly, the emotional consequences of the election varied across these groups. The long-term members, who have used the forum for a significant period, were affected in a different way by the election and expressed less intense emotions. In contrast, new members exhibited strong emotions of desperation, disgust, and shock. To examine these processes in more detail, we compare how these groups expressed themselves in their posts following the election, focusing on both the content of the posts and the level of sentiments. Specifically, we scrutinize the content of these emotional expression. However, we begin by dissecting user activity based on user groups.

Over the years, Stormfront has been increasingly dominated by long-term users who are more active on the forum and drive the posting activity, compared to new users (see Figure 7.1). This pattern was also largely visible after the Obama 2008 election, as the majority of posts after the election were posted by established, long-term members. However, while older posters were prevalent in terms of the number of posts, the election also brought a new influx of contributors to the forum.

Given the unprecedented rise in new members to the forum and the fact that this user group was also significantly more active than before, this implies that the election had a unique impact on these users. To further investigate this, we focus on the content of the posts in the wake of the election to comprehend the significance of this event for the community members. The objective of this analysis is to gain insights into the underlying cognitive and emotional mechanisms through which identity threats and traumas affect the members. We anticipate that different groups within a movement possess varying abilities and capacities to cope with traumatic events. To study this, we constructed two sub-corpora. The first included all posts on the forum in a two-week period after the 2008 election that were posted by members who registered during the same period (N=3,130). This period was chosen to capture the activity of new users on the platform. The second subcorpus included all posts by long-term members, defined as those who had contributed to the forum for more than 12 months and written at least 50 posts, that were posted during the same period (N=24,804). This allows us to compare the content of the posts by new users and long-term members of the community. Additionally, this enables us to explore the emotions expressed by different members in the wake of the election, as well as the rationales and motivations they provide for joining the forum.

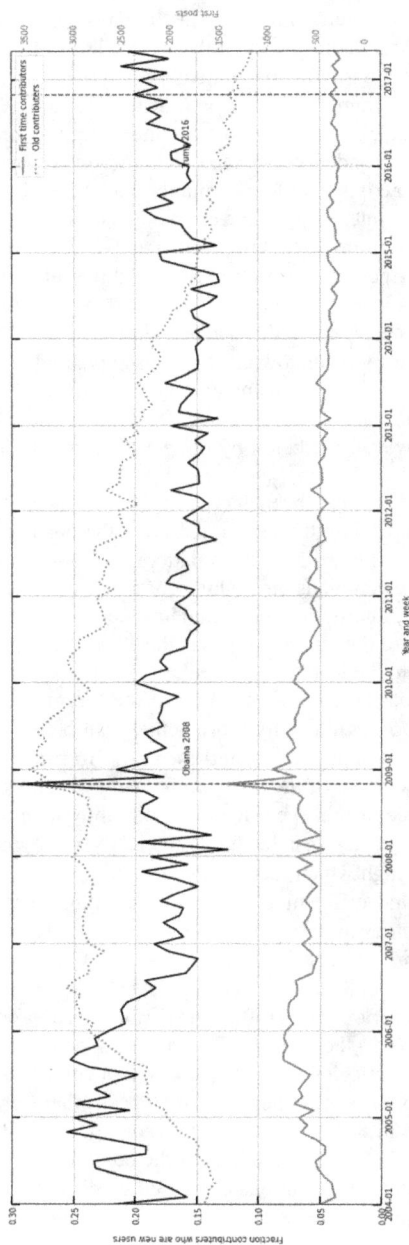

Figure 7.1 The figure shows the number of monthly contributors split by whether the month marked their first contribution or not. The dotted gray line shows the number of old contributors, while the gray line in the bottom shows the number of contributors who is contributing for the first time. The black line shows the fraction of the members contributing during the week that were contributing for the first time. As the graph shows, while there was a surge in the activity of long-term members, the election of Obama in 2008 also resulted in an even larger surge in contributions from members who had not previously posted on the forum, increasing from 15–20% to 30% of the active members in that month.

Long-term Members

Figures 7.2 and 7.3 demonstrate the main differences in the response of long-term members and new members to the election of Obama. The networks depict the word collocations that were most distinctive in each sub-corpus, represented as discursive networks.[1]

One of the most striking findings is that long-term members seem to have a relatively established sense of collective identity, as demonstrated by a strong focus on the in-group, particularly through the use of word collocations containing "we". Some examples include "We Whites", "We nationalists", "We fighting, "We act", and "We want".

This finding seems to partially diverge from the results discussed in Chapter 5, where users over time, did in fact not appear to use the term "we" more frequently but instead preferred to use internal terms to denote in-group belonging. For instance, we observed a transition from "my" and "I" to "your" and increased usage of specific terms like "WN" and "SF".

That the same patterns are not reflected in the period immediately following the election of Obama appears to stem from the significant influx of new users, leading long-standing members to address a new audience, thus shifting to more welcoming and inclusive language. This is reinforced by our

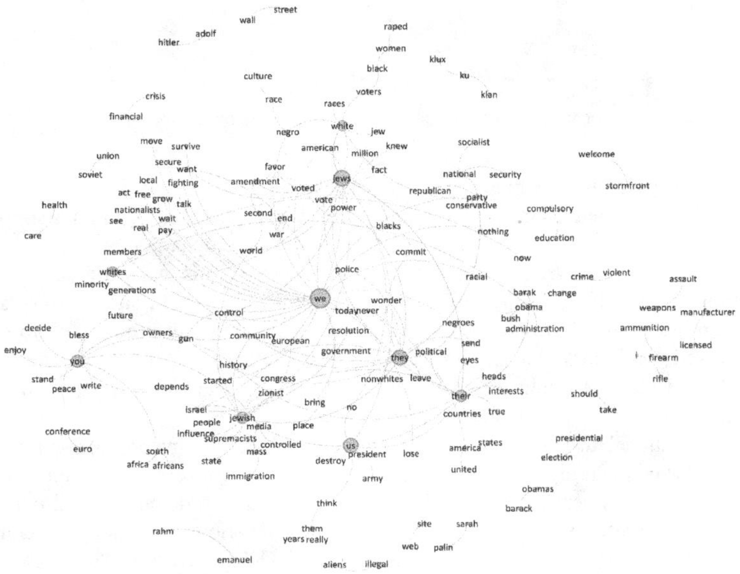

Figure 7.2 Collocation network of posts by long-term members on the forum. The figure shows word bigrams that are overrepresented in the corpus.

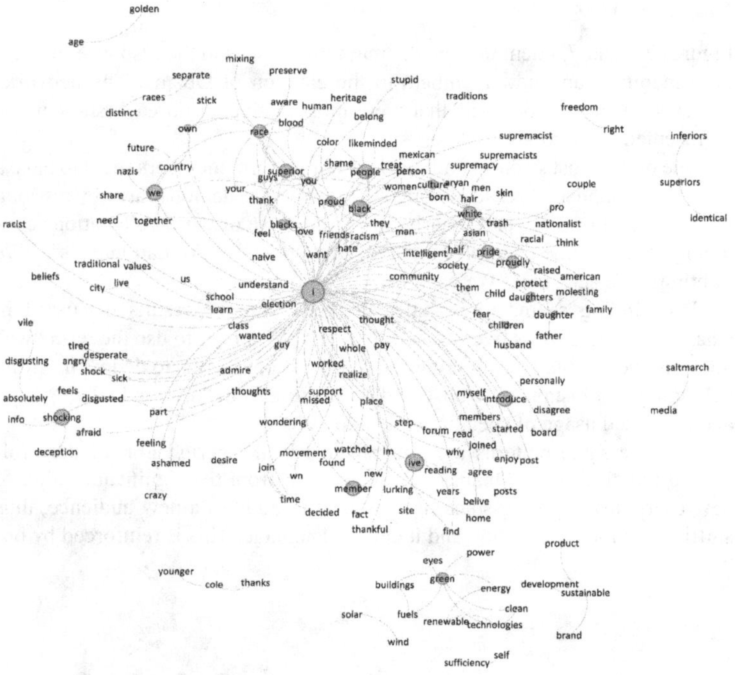

Figure 7.3 Collocation network of posts by new members on the forum.

qualitative analysis, which reveals that a substantial portion of posts from the more established users explicitly target new forum members, and an associated tendency to reduce the usage of community-specific jargon.

Moreover, the frequent use of derogatory expressions and word collocations designating an out-group suggest a clear sense of enemy and us versus them mentality. Jews are clearly identified as the main out-group, with top-ranked word pairs such as "Jews their", "Jewish media", "Jewish influence", "Jews us", "Jews control", etc. These results align well with our previous findings, as demonstrated in Chapter 5.

Additional distinguishing features of this sub-corpus include a focus on broader political topics, such as the Second Amendment (e.g., "voted amendment", "gun owners", "firearm ammunition", "second amendment"), but also the financial crisis, Wall Street, illegal immigration, and various political figures and groups, such as Sarah Palin, Rahm Emanuel, and KKK. There is also a tendency to use derogatory expressions like "negroes" and "niggers". Overall, these patterns are further supported by the top-ranked single words in this corpus, which are dominated by "Jewish", "Jew", "negroes", "amendment", "gun", and "rifle".

New Members

In contrast to long-term members, new members were less inclined to identify themselves with a clearly defined in-group, as the absence of "we" in word collocations indicates (Figure 7.3). Rather, they describe themselves as individuals belonging to a broader category or a certain ethnic group, suggested by that the single most frequent word collocation in this corpus is "I White", followed by "I American//people/nationalist/race/country". There also appears to be a stronger tendency among these members to express their personal opinion ("I believe/think/agree/disagree/values/desire"). Interestingly, there may also be a tendency among new members to focus on green sustainability ("renewable technology/energy", "green buildings", "green fuels", etc.).

The sub-corpus is characterized by the overrepresentation of various emotional expressions, particularly feelings of "desperation", "shock", "sickness", "disgust", "hate", "vile", and "fear". This pattern is further supported when examining single words, revealing a high (relative) frequency of strong emotional words. Another distinctive pattern are bigrams that indicate feelings of racial pride, with common word collocations such as "superior race", "proud white", "white pride", and "racial pride". Instead of Jews being the main out-group, new members seem to focus mainly on racial issues concerning Black persons. There are, in fact, no highly ranked words or word pairs relating to Jews in the sub-corpus.

In addition, there are two distinctive clusters of word collocations in this sub-corpus. The first concerns various family-oriented words such as "husband children", "I father", "I husband", "white father", "child I", and "husband I". "I daughter", "my wife", and "fear children". The second cluster includes words that seem to concern the motivations of these members to join the forum. For instance, "I've lurking/reading/years", "likeminded people", "I friends", "identical superiors", "own people", "white friends", "stick own". The analysis above has revealed the broader patterns distinguishing each corpus. In the next section, we attempt to extend, validate, and begin to explain these patterns by employing sentiment analysis combined with qualitative text analysis.

Sentiments and Emotional Expressions

To analyze the sentiments expressed by new users and long-term users, we used the Vader sentiment analysis model, which is designed specifically for social media texts (Hutto & Gilbert, 2014). This lexicon-based model is sensitive to both the polarity and intensity of sentiments. For this step, we used the same subcorpora as for the analysis above, but this time, we only included posts that contained keywords relating to Obama, allowing us to focus on the sentiments that were specifically related to the election.[2]

The results of the sentiment analysis show that new users tend to use significantly more emotional expressions than long-term users in the period following the election (see Figure 7.4).[3] This trend is evident in both positive

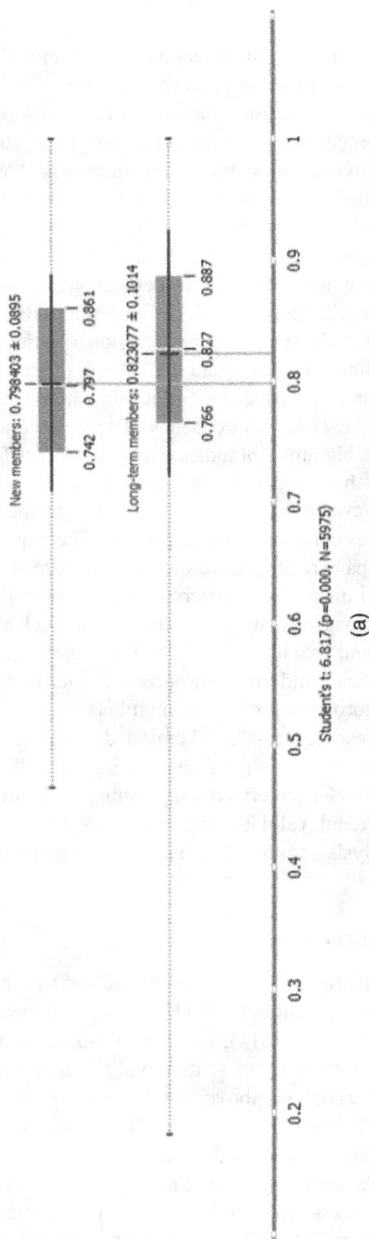

New members: 0.798403 ± 0.0895

0.742   0.797   0.861

Long-term members: 0.823077 ± 0.1014

0.766   0.827   0.887

Student's t: 6.817 (p=0.000, N=5975)

(a)

Figure 7.4 These graphs depict emotional expressions among different user groups. The left vertical line through the box indicates the median, representing the 50th percentile. The right vertical line represents the mean. The box's left boundary marks the 25th percentile, and the right boundary indicates the 75th percentile. Whiskers extend to cover the full range of variance. (a) Neutral sentiments, (b) positive sentiments, and (c) negative sentiments. *(Continued)*

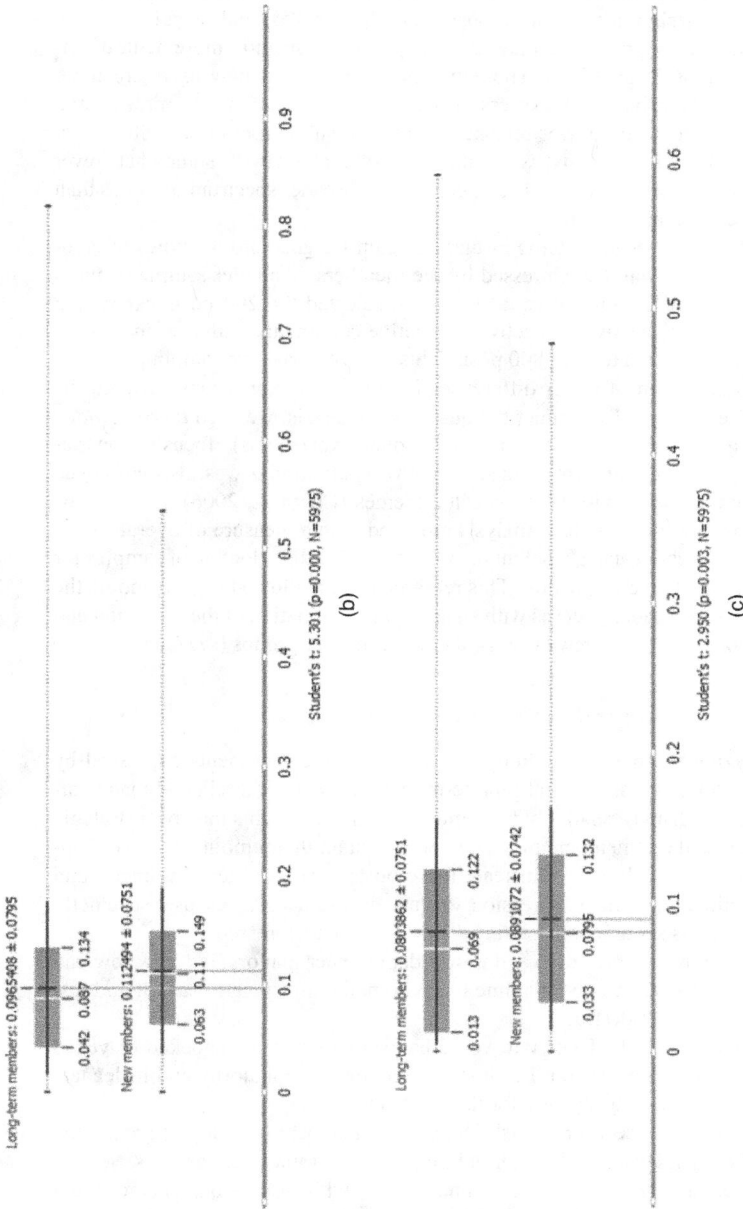

Long-term members:: 0.0965408 ± 0.0795

0.042 0.087 0.134

New members:: 0.112494 ± 0.0751

0.063 0.11 0.149

Student's t: 5.301 (p=0.000, N=5975)

(b)

Long-term members:: 0.0803862 ± 0.0751

0.013 0.069 0.122

New members:: 0.0891072 ± 0.0742

0.033 0.0795 0.132

Student's t: 2.950 (p=0.003, N=5975)

(c)

Figure 7.4 (Continued)

and negative emotions. Statistical analysis using t-tests[4] shows that new users express significantly more positive (5.3, p: 0.000) and negative (2.950, p: 0.003) emotions, while older users express significantly more neutral sentiments (6.817, p: 0.000). These findings suggest that new users are more emotionally driven and express stronger sentiments about the presidential election. The analysis was repeated on the full sub-corpora (i.e., without using the list of keywords) with similar results, albeit with somewhat lower values, as expected since this corpus covers a broader spectrum of topics than the presidential election.

To explore these patterns further and gain insights into the types of emotions and motivations expressed by the members, a smaller sample of posts was selected for qualitative analysis. We selected the 200 posts expressing the strongest positive respectively negative sentiments within each subcorpus, resulting in a total of 800 posts. This type of purposive sampling enabled the examination of major differences in emotional expressions between the two user groups. To conduct the qualitative analysis, we used *theory-guided coding* (focusing on nuances in emotional expressions), focusing on nuances in emotional expressions. *Inductive open coding* was also employed to maintain sensitivity to unexpected themes (Charmaz, 2006). In this way, the quantitative sentiment analysis provided both a measure of overall sentiments expressed and a "content map" that enabled the selection of samples for closer qualitative inspection. This research design allowed us to combine the analysis of broader patterns with an in-depth examination of the reasoning and emotions behind the responses of the different user groups (see Chapter 3).

Long-term Members' Emotional Expressions

Analyzing the posts containing the most negative sentiments expressed by long-term users, shows that long-term members exhibit a relatively jaded attitude and display relatively few emotional outbursts. This may be a strategic choice, as these members may attempt to contain their emotions to avoid appearing politically naive. Instead, these posts express bitterness, anger, and frustration, rather than depression, disgust, or disgrace. As one user succinctly captures this sentiment by stating: "I'm upset, not depressed".

First a Negro president and now a damn queer mayor. God how low can these fools get?! Maybe it's time to say to hell with trying to save it and just let America self-destruct.

This is horrible, I knew it would happen so I was not shocked or vexed to the point of frustration; I'm just sad that the white majority and its leaders have lost pride and any care for their heritage.

As we have seen previously, long-term members typically approach the election by focusing on broader political issues or topics such as Jews, Second Amendment rights, and international issues, with discussions characterized by relatively neutral parlance (in the context of a far-right forum). They view the election as an unfortunate and regrettable event, but not unexpected, and rather a predictable result of the "prevailing Jewish order".

Are we losing sight of the fact that Obama is just a figurehead puppet? Do you really think that Obama controls anything? International Jewry is the greatest threat, hands down. Obama is an impotent house negro, nothing more.

When examining the most positive posts within this sub-corpus, they often contain a high degree of irony and sarcasm. For instance: "Exposure to diversity is the surest cure for tolerance. I'm glad Obama won". Such expressions are more common among established members compared to new members. Additionally, other positive posts include friendly and inviting posts, welcoming new members to the community, and expressing general optimism about the large influx of new members to both the community and the white nationalist movement overall. In this way, older members attempt to create effective bonds with the newcomers: "I'm glad to see many new members! Welcome to SF!"

Overall, the analysis suggests that the election of Obama was not a significant disruptive event or a moral shock for the long-term members of the forum. These individuals already had well-established grievances and the event did not challenge their identities or force them to reconsider basic beliefs. Instead, the election of Obama allowed long-term users to enforce their worldviews, strengthen their solidarity, and their sense of "we-ness".

New Members' Emotional Expressions

In contrast, the election was a shocking event for new members of the community, who expressed intense emotions and profusely discussed their feelings, which resembled a form of emotional venting.

I'm even too shocked to feel sick or disgusted. It's a scary time for the white race, scarier than ever before… Right now, I think my mind is a blur of emotions, and I can't think logically about how this situation might be fixed.

As the sentiment analysis illustrated, new members express intense positive *and* negative emotions. At first sight, this may appear contradictory. Looking at the 200 most negative posts in this sub-corpus, a broad spectrum of emotions, including fear, resignation, despair, shame, disgust, and depression, were expressed, but also to some extent frustration and anger. Shame, disgust, and nausea are particularly common, with expressions such as: "Last night made me sick to my stomach"; "I'm heartsick and saddened"; "I vomit in my mouth a bit"; "I want to puke". Overall, words like disgrace, disgusting, despicable, shocking, and sickening stand out as particularly common, which was also evident in the z-test. These types of "visceral, bodily feelings, on a par with vertigo or nausea" are commonly associated with moral shocks (Goodwin et al., 2009, p. 16).

Emotions of disgust, shame, and disgrace were typically expressed by the new members as a reaction to the fact that a person belonging to an alleged "inferior" race won the presidential election and that white people now are "subordinated to Blacks". As illustrated by the two following posts, many members describe it as particularly upsetting and "disgraceful" that a Black person will now occupy the same position as a series of "dignified" white presidents before him.

The national disgrace! To elect a representative of a sub-human black race that is so hostile and hateful to the white people; that is the ENEMY of the white people; that is despicable and disgusting; that is so inferior to the white people; that is so destructive to the society; that never belonged among the white people. Shame on you!

To think that Barack Hussein Obama will join the likes of FDR, Eisenhower, Washington, Jefferson, and Reagan, is an absolute disgrace to those men of great stature and noble bloodline. Makes me want to fuc**ng puke.

Many new members struggled to cope with the contradiction that a person belonging to an alleged "inferior" race could hold a position of power and framed the election as a threat to the white race, expressing fears of becoming a minority and being discriminated against. While long-term members solved this apparent contradiction by focusing on Jews as the main target and out-group (and Obama was thus merely seen as a "Jewish puppet"), the new members primarily identified race as the main concern, with Black people being the most distinguished out-group. The election, therefore, posed a fundamental challenge to the new members, who based their identity and self-value on social comparison with other races and devaluation of Black people.

The election is repeatedly and explicitly described as a turning point for new members of the forum, influencing their decision to register and become active in the community. Many expressed a need to "take action" and "do something" in response to the event, but also a desire for comfort, moral support, and a way to make sense of their upset. For instance: "I have been reading for some time, but this was the final tipping point, I felt compelled to register and post"; "over the years my concerns has grown this was a tipping point". The elections served as a moral shock that motivated these individuals to join the community, and they often cited concerns about the safety of their families, particularly their daughters and children, as a reason for their involvement.

I just found this site and joined right away. I just want to say I am afraid of what is happening in America. I have three children and I am scared to death ... They will breed with our daughters until our blood no longer runs pure and we will be gone.

Shared Emotions: Transforming Dread into Outrage

Emotions are not just instinctive reactions to external events. Movements are themselves also a distinct setting in which emotions can be created or reinforced. Many members shared personal stories of past injustices, alleged oppression, offenses, assaults, and violence allegedly performed by Black people, which served to fuel a sense of moral outrage. These stories often include an idealized victim, such as a young woman or daughter, who has allegedly been assaulted. For instance:

> Last night made me so sick to my stomach. One of my female friends was robbed of all her things. I saw black teens harassing white cops, saying they aren't **** and don't matter. I think I vomited in my mouth.

Such stories represent what Jasper refers to as *shared emotions* and reflect how new members of the community collectively nurture anger and outrage toward outsiders. They identify concrete and specific adversaries, thus turning attention from the specific "disaster" of a member of an "inferior race" winning the election and the resulting feelings of grief and despair to focusing instead on the corruption and dangerous nature of their enemies – thus enhancing the protestor's sense of threat. In this way, the indignities of daily life are transformed into a shared grievance with a focused target of collective action. According to Gamson (1992), to sustain collective action, the targets identified by the frame must successfully bridge the abstract and the concrete. This process is particularly evident in some of these narratives: while the stories depict concrete and actual events that involve Black people, at the same time, they emphasize that violence and immoral acts are embedded in their very nature as Black people. In this way, the members connect broader sociocultural forces with human agents who are appropriate targets of collective action.

Through cognitive reframing, the members transform passive emotions, such as dread, hopelessness, fear, resignation, shame, and disgust, into active emotions, such as moral indignation and outrage, which provide better and more stable grounds for both action and collective identity. While resignation can dampen perceived opportunity for change, emotions such as anger, indignation, and pride are commonly associated with political agency (Jasper, 2011). In contrast, the established, long-term members do not need this: their grievances are firmly established – they are already angry and emotionally charged for action.

Reciprocal Emotions: Nurturing a Collective Identity

Examining the 200 posts by new members that are classified as most positive, these can be broadly sorted into two categories: [i] personal presentations where members describe themselves, and [ii] affective emotions relating to their experiences of social bonding, togetherness, and social support.

In the former category, new members present themselves to the community, describing themselves as "proud whites" and expressing pride in belonging to a "superior race". This tendency to emphasize pride was also evident in the quantitative analysis and may have served to transform deactivating emotions, such as shame or depression, into activating emotions, such as anger, outrage, and indignation, which encourage action. Pride and shame are moral emotions of self-approval or self-disapproval that involve a feeling of connection or disconnection from one's social bonds, and emphasizing pride and superiority may serve to further strengthen a sense of community among the members.

The second category of positive posts included various expressions of social bonding and support, which can be conceptualized as *reciprocal emotions*. Members thank each other for receiving support and being welcomed to the forum. Many claim that the reason for joining the forum was to find moral and social support and a protected space to discuss with like-minded people. As one user puts it: "I came here to converse and find solidarity with fellow White Nationalists".

According to Collins, participation in these positively toned gatherings reinforces common identity and personal and collective self-esteem – similar to de Koster and Houtman (2008) emphasis on messages as sources of sociability, resulting in communal solidarity. Collective identity refers to both a process and a product. On the most basic level, it is the process by which individuals come to see themselves in others; the product is a common understanding of "we", or seeing the "we" in "me" (Melucci, 1989; Touraine, 1985). Through these posts and the succeeding discussions, members create personal bonds of friendship and loyalty and enhance feelings of trust and solidarity. For instance, as expressed in these two posts: "I'd just like to thank everyone for responding to my posts and for the most part being respectful"; "Very happy to have joined SF, glad to have joined this site, the election has fired up my desire to reach out to other whites".

The election of Obama thus became a combative issue that contributed to the energy and solidarity of the community. As Collins states, this process of emotional arousal and shared emotions, driven by a moral shock or other events, tends to occur over limited time periods. Typically, their peaks are only sustainable for a few days. This corresponds well with user activity on the forum: the sharp peak with many new members and high posting activity only lasts for a limited time.

Conclusion

This chapter has highlighted how cultural trauma – that is, an experience of unrooting from the narrative web that situates us in our community – is key to driving individuals to join online communities like Stormfront. These communities, in turn, afford processes involving both the creation and dissemination of trauma narratives that offer meaning to – and hence enable the processing of – feelings of fear, anxiety, and despair. Such narratives assist individuals in making sense of what is happening by telling a story in which the event can be made compatible with and slotted into a larger structure of understanding – processing what occurred and who is responsible. Furthermore, the social process of generating these narratives may also serve to transform passive feelings into emotional energy and a sense of collective identity. The Durkheimian process of ritualistic interaction, as extended and elaborated by Collins, allows individuals to come together to face their traumas, find comfort and support, and construct new narratives that embed them in new communities.

The empirical analysis has revealed that different groups of users within the Stormfront community were differentially affected by the election of Obama, as they had access to different coping mechanisms in response to this event. New members experienced the election as a traumatic moral shock, expressing intense emotions of shame, resignation, and disgust in their posts immediately following the election. Many of these members joined Stormfront as a means of processing this traumatic experience, seeking meaning and social and moral support from like-minded individuals. Once part of the community, they engaged in the development of new (trauma) narratives to provide coherence and meaning to the situation, sharing personalized stories that cast the general shock as a concrete enemy and justified moral outrage by revealing the "corrupt" and "dangerous" nature of Black people.

By supporting and encouraging each other (reciprocal emotions) and collectively diagnosing and describing shared injustices and grievances (shared emotions), the two types of collective emotions merged in the discussions. In this experience of emotional communion, passive and individual emotions become fused into a collective emotion, creating a shared sense of identity and a drive for collective action. The social rituals of narrative construction that developed in the community served as the social glue that bound members together, increased solidarity, motivated individuals to remain active, and provided a foundation for the construction of a collective identity. It is worth noting that the rituals of narrative construction were collective, bottom-up processes that involved many members rather than being strategically shaped by individual leaders as sometimes described in the literature on framing and moral shock (Williams, 2004).

Feelings of shame, despair, depression, and disgust are thus transformed into solidarity in the community. They felt one with the community. The undefined sense of difference was replaced by an articulated belief in the superiority of the White race. They were the heroes of their stories once again. In this experience of emotional communion, individuals form a sense of social belonging and shared beliefs. Pain turned into anger. Hatred. As Baldwin once put it, "I imagine that one of the reasons that people cling to their hates so stubbornly is because they sense, once hate is gone, that they will be forced to deal with pain". Their passive feelings could turn into active feelings. Determination. Strength. Self-confidence.

In contrast, long-term members of Stormfront reacted very differently to the election. While their activity in the community increased in the immediate aftermath of the election, these members exhibited less strong emotional out-bursts. They did not experience the election as a moral shock: it did not pose a significant threat to their worldviews or their identities. They already had a narrative in place for making sense of the election of a Black president – centered on the belief of Jews as the scheming masterminds, while casting Obama as merely another Black "puppet" – hence protecting and leaving intact their inherent sense of supremacy as white Americans. This suggests that strong ties and social and discursive immersion in a community can, in certain situations, serve as a shock absorber that protects individuals from the negative effects of traumatic events.

Online communities like Stormfront, therefore, not only provide a platform for the far right to express contentious opinions and ideas (Koster & Houtman, 2008), but they also serve as a form of "emotional refuge" (Reddy, 2001): a space for collective emotional work where members can express and collectively interpret feelings and emotional responses in ways that would not be accepted in mainstream society. While previous research has emphasized the role of sociability and interaction in fostering a sense of community on social media, these results accentuate these communities' central function in facilitating the *emotional* processes that transform a set of individuals into a community and a community into an active political entity. This speaks to Ganesh's (2018, pp. 33–34) suggestion that, for the far right, what unites communities online are "forms of intimacy, sense, and feeling that are maligned or considered unacceptable in mainstream society".

Notes

1 The word collocations were calculated using z-tests, which are statistical tests for comparing the means of two large samples when the variances are known. This allowed us to identify words and bigrams that were statistically over- and under-represented in each subcorpus (excluding stop words). We then used social network analysis to illustrate the resulting word collocations.

2 The keywords are the following: Obama, Obongo, president*, white_house, Osama, election, elected, leader, joined, join, new member, last night, obamination, win, and register (N: 5975). This list of keywords was created iteratively by identifying words that were commonly used in relation to the election.

3 Noticeably, this runs counter to the overall patterns on the forum, as users generally tend to express more negative sentiments over time.

4 Student-t or t-test assesses the statistical significance of the difference between two sample means.

References

Alexander, J. C. (2004). Toward a theory of cultural trauma. In J. C. Alexander, R. Eyerman, B. Giesen, N. Smelser, & P. Sztompka (Eds.), *Cultural trauma and collective identity*. Berkeley: University of California Press.

Caruth, C. (2016). *Unclaimed experience: Trauma, narrative, and history*. New York: JHU Press.

Charmaz, K. (2006). *Constructing grounded theory: A practical guide through qualitative analysis*. New York: Sage.

Collins, R. (2004). *Interaction ritual chains*. Princeton: Princeton University Press.

Collins, R. (2009). Social movements and the focus of emotional attention. In J. Goodwin, J. Jasper, & F. Polletta (Eds.), *Passionate politics: Emotions and social movements* (pp. 27–44). Chicago: University of Chicago Press.

Durkheim, E. (1912). *Elementary forms of the religious life*. London: George Allen & Unwin Ltd.

Eyerman, R. (2004). Cultural trauma: Slavery and the formation of African American identity. In J. C. Alexander (Ed.), *Cultural trauma and collective identity* (pp. 60–111). Berkeley: University of California Press.

Eyerman, R. (2022). *The making of White American identity*. London: Oxford University Press.

Gamson, W. A. (1992). *Talking politics*. Cambridge: Cambridge University Press.

Ganesh, B. (2018). The ungovernability of digital hate culture. *Journal of international affairs*, 71(2), 30–49.

Goodwin, J. (1997). The libidinal constitution of a high-risk social movement: Affectual ties and solidarity in the Huk rebellion, 1946 to 1954. *American sociological review*, 62(1), 53–69.

Goodwin, J., Jasper, J. M., & Polletta, F. (2009). *Passionate politics: Emotions and social movements*. Chicago: University of Chicago Press.

Hutto, C., & Gilbert, E. (2014). Vader: A parsimonious rule-based model for sentiment analysis of social media text. In *Proceedings of the international AAAI conference on web and social media* (Vol. 8, No. 1, pp. 216–225).

Jasper, J. (1998). *The emotions of protest: Affective and reactive emotions in and around social movements*. Paper presented at the Sociological Forum.

Jasper, J. (2008). *The art of moral protest: Culture, biography, and creativity in social movements*. Chicago: University of Chicago Press.

Jasper, J. (2011). Emotions and social movements: Twenty years of theory and research. *Annual review of sociology*, 37(1), 285–303. https://doi.org/10.1146/annurev-soc-081309-150015

Koster, W., & Houtman, D. (2008). Stormfront is like a second home to me: On virtual community formation by right-wing extremists. *Information, communication and society*, 11(8), 1155–1176.

LaCapra, D. (2014). *Writing history, writing trauma*. New York: JHU Press.

McAdam, D. (1982). *Political process and the development of black insurgency, 1930-1970*. Chicago: University of Chicago Press.

Melucci, A. (1989). *Nomads of the present: Social movements and individual needs in contemporary society*. New York: Vintage.

Reddy, W. (2001). *The navigation of feeling: A framework for the history of emotions*. Cambridge: Cambridge University Press.

Smith, P. (2010). *Why war?: The cultural logic of Iraq, the Gulf War, and Suez*. Chicago: University of Chicago Press.

Snow, D., Cress, D., Downey, L., & Jones, A. (1998). Disrupting the "quotidian": Reconceptualizing the relationship between breakdown and the emergence of collective action. *Mobilization: An international quarterly*, 3(1), 1–22.

Smelser, N. J. (2004). Psychological trauma and cultural trauma. In J. C. Alexander (Ed.), *Cultural trauma and collective identity, 4th ed* (pp. 31–59). Berkeley: University of California Press.

Snow, D., & Soule, S. (2010). *A primer on social movements.* New York: W. W. Norton.

Sztompka, P. (2004). The trauma of social change. In J. C. Alexander (Ed.), *Cultural trauma and collective identity* (pp. 60–111). Berkeley: University of California Press.

Touraine, A. (1985). An introduction to the study of social movements. *Social research*, 54(4), 749–787.

Warren, M. R. (2010). *Fire in the heart: How white activists embrace racial justice.* Oxford: Oxford University Press.

Williams, R. (2004). The cultural contexts of collective action: Constraints, opportunities, and the symbolic life of social movements. In D. Snow, S. Soule, & H. Kriesi (Eds.), *The Blackwell companion to social movements* (pp. 91–115). London: Blackwell.

8 Stormfront and the Rise of the Far Right

Social media has reshaped the very fabric of extremist mobilization and radicalization over the past two decades. Radicalization has, in some sense, become an online phenomenon as digital spaces have come to replace formal organizations, redefining the mechanisms of violence and the pathways to extremism.

As a result of these transformations, the boundaries between mainstream politics and extremist movements have been redrawn – becoming blurred and ill-defined. In the United States, a concerning 20% of the population perceive political violence as legitimate, and 7.1% say that they would be willing to kill a person to advance their political agendas (Wintemute et al., 2022). Mainstream politicians adeptly use social media, tapping into and fueling a movement base that bolsters their political coalitions. Extremism has, in short, gone mainstream.

While it is now widely agreed among researchers that social media is at the core of contemporary forms of political radicalization, our understanding of the underlying causal link between social media and political extremism remains superficial. As we have seen, the concept of the "echo chamber" has come to serve as the go-to explanation for the link between social media and radicalization, arguing that the internet allows us to immerse ourselves in our own political fantasies, free from judgment or exposure to counterarguments. As we are constantly exposed to one-sided arguments, the argument goes, we become increasingly radical in our convictions.

The echo chamber hypothesis thus implicitly casts politics as principally about opinions, portraying social media as a sphere for deliberation and the exchange of rational arguments. This perspective belongs to the so-called "folk theory" of democracy, where politics progress from rational debate to policy preferences, ultimately selecting the party or movement that best mirrors these policy positions (Achen & Bartels, 2017). This theory perceives politics as a purely rational affair, confined to arguments, opinions, and policies. Democracy is said to function as long as we maintain a unified public sphere in which we can come together to debate, work out our differences, and arrive at a common viewpoint. Consequently, the current surge

DOI: 10.4324/9781003108344-9

in radicalization and polarization is seen as stemming from the collapse of this public sphere, with digitalization causing a fragmentation that no longer forces us to engage with opposing perspectives.

In this book, we have challenged not only the echo chamber hypothesis but also the entire premise of this debate. Politics, we have argued, has never been merely about opinions and policy and has always encompassed more than just arguments and debates: things like identity, emotion, and sense of belonging. The fabric of political life is not purely about rational exchanges or arguments: as its core, it is profoundly *social*.

To understand radicalization and far-right movements, we have argued that we are better off inverting the causal arrow of the "folk theory" of politics: viewing politics as originating from identity and political belonging, which leads to taking up opinions and policy positions from our social community, and then finally inventing *post hoc* rationalizations and arguments for why these opinions are true (Törnberg et al., 2021). While we may, over time, construct opinions, ideologies, and sophisticated arguments that justify our political identities, these are seldom fundamental. The core unit of this form of political life is not the exchange of rational arguments but rather *rituals* – activities that operate in the realm of community, emotion, identity, and belonging.

Politics thus straddles two realms – it has one foot in rationality and arguments and the other in tribes, rituals, and emotions. As this book has served to argue, the structure and activities of our public sphere are key to determining which of these realms gain primacy in our political life. This theoretical lens suggests a new way of understanding the impact of social media and digitalization.

Rather than the dominant emphasis on arguments as the core element of politics, this book has thus developed a Durkheimian understanding of online political engagement as rooted in rituals. Where the Habermasian view of the public draws on the image of the rational debates of the European coffeehouses, Durkheim's theory is modeled on the social life of Aboriginal tribes: communal gatherings around campfires, involving rhythmic dancing and chanting, fostering a sense of belonging that concurrently nurtures an associated community culture. In this context, online communities like Stormfront are better understood through the lenses of rituals and identity rather than arguments and rationality. While some interactions may take the form of arguments and reasoning, these are seldom fundamental: the messages chiefly serve as symbolic identity markers. Much like Aboriginal chanting, the words are less important than the rhythm, the feeling, and the sense of shared activity.

The Durkheimian theory of the social dimensions of political life illuminates not only the dynamics of digital spaces such as Stormfront but also extends to the 18th-century coffeehouses that influenced Habermas' conceptualization of the public sphere. This understanding of the nature and function of meeting places in political life fundamentally recasts our understanding of the impact of digitalization. Digitalization did not undermine rational debate by shattering and fragmenting a unified space of public debate into isolated echo chambers; the public sphere was always fragmented. Instead, the impact of digitalization becomes a question of enabling and empowering distinct forms of politics. Digitalization appears to have fueled an identity-based form of politics by altering the dynamics, scale, and nature of these Durkheimian processes. It has, in short, shifted the balance between the two realms of political life – moving our body politics to slant dangerously towards the tribal.

How, then, do we understand these tribal consequences of the internet and social media? Why did these forms of communication tilt the balance between rituals and rational exchange?

To understand this, we can revisit the optimistic narratives surrounding the advent of the early internet with which we began this book. As early internet scholars argued, the internet would herald a new era of democratization by enabling new forms of political participation. It would remove gatekeepers, reduce the costs of participation, and enable disenfranchised and minority groups more intense participation in political life. As nearly anyone would be able to create a new digital meeting space, minority groups would be put on near-equal footing with wealthy and powerful media empires. By concealing the identity of our interlocutors, the internet was to foster a color and gender-blind form of politics and enable more fluid ways of relating to our identities. We would become active participants in political debate, not merely passive receivers of political discourse, and the public sphere would thus again become truly public, granting nearly anyone the chance to participate.

While their optimism was perhaps naïve, these scholars were not wrong with regard to the specific points: many of these expectations indeed came true. But they did not usher in the expected democratic renaissance. If these points were realized in a Habermasian world in which politics is merely about opinions and issue positions, and the public sphere is about deliberation and arguments, then we would indeed expect a new era of democratization. But in a world where politics has its second foot rooted in the realm of emotion and identity, and the public sphere gives space also for rituals and communities, then the result of these points will be profoundly different. Since the public sphere was never solely about critical-rational debate, their ramifications were profoundly different from what their theorists envisioned.

First, the removal of gatekeepers may have facilitated participation by disenfranchised groups, but it also inadvertently empowered violent extremist fractions. While granting a platform for well-overdue grievances from excluded groups, it also opened the floodgates for racial resentment and extremist discourse. The undeniably problematic powers of the gatekeepers of traditional media to determine what issues and groups were allowed into the realm of political debate were employed not only to exclude minority voices but also to suppress calls for violence and racial resentment. As these gate-keepers were disempowered, the boundary between legitimate discourse and that which lies outside the acceptable was blurred or even erased.

Second, the lowering of the costs of creating political meeting spaces may indeed have produced arenas in which oppressed minority groups can find solace in community and shared experiences. However, it also enabled similar processes among fringe far-right extremists. Historically, setting up a politi-cal meeting place – be it a White Power concert or a cross-burning – required some level of organizational work and institutional structures. Even the most rabidly violent extremists needed to labor in the mundane realm of political organizing – schedule bi-weekly meetings to organize a venue, discuss financ-ing, the poster design, and PR, and naturally, someone would need to chair meetings, take notes, and preferably bring coffee and biscuits. This not only limited the frequency of such events but also meant that the energy gener-ated from the events was channeled into these formal organizations and the hierarchies they generated. But social media has made the creation of political meeting spaces trivial: a Facebook or WhatsApp group can be set up within minutes. As a result, the energy generated is no longer necessarily channeled into formal organizations but instead often feeds a spontaneous and uncon-trolled form of mobilization. While there are still leaders – indeed, the move-ments can be highly centralized around specific individuals, as exemplified by QAnon – these often do not hold formal roles within any institutional struc-ture. Digitalization has resulted in movements becoming more fragmented and distributed, constituted by chains of rituals without formal organization and institutional structures to channel and direct their action. Consequently, movement energy is channeled not into institutional work based on strategic political consideration but into more chaotic, unpredictable, and often violent political action.

Third, while social media in part concealed the visible identities of our interlocutors, this did not result in the predicted race- and gender-blind public sphere, nor in more fluid relationships to our identities. Instead, the locus of identity work shifted from outward appearances to the realm of language and discourse. While the extremism of old was seen in particular cloth-ing or apparel – ranging from white robes to bomber jackets and shaved heads – the extremism of today is expressed through words, phrases, memes, and symbols – such as marking enemies by ((((parenthesis)))) or turning some-thing as innocuous as milk into a symbol of white supremacy. Within political movements, group affiliation is now expressed through memes and language games, in which belonging is conveyed by the capacity to navigate complex discursive systems. These discursive expressions of identity can spread like wildfire through public discourse, quickly making their way from fringe ex-tremist spaces to mainstream media – and, in the process, bringing with them their ideological content and worldviews.

Finally, by lowering the thresholds for participation, digital media did bring broader participation in political life: it turned many from passive receivers to active participants in political discussions. But the resultant politics were not chiefly a politics of rational deliberation. As this book has argued, the shift from passive to active engagement brings with it a shift in how we experience and relate to politics. There are fundamental differences in the effects of passive consumption and active participation.

While the echo chamber hypothesis of radicalization may focus on the effects of reading and consuming what other people post, the perspective developed in this book focuses on *participation* – engaging in conversation and posting, sharing stories and anecdotes – as the key locus of radicalization. Reading and consuming stories around a topic – whether through newspapers, television, or on social media – may lead us to build interest and even opinions about the given topic. Watching cooking shows on television, for instance, will often make us more interested in cooking, and we may learn and form opinions about – say – the benefits of cast iron pans over Teflon. But it does not in itself produce a community. In contrast, when we participate and engage in conversation online, it affects us on the level of identity and emotion: it transforms that interest into a nascent identity. On social media platforms, even something as tame as cooking can bring about separations into *us* and *them*. Take the fundamentalists of the cast iron cooking community on Reddit, with their unquestioning love for multi-layered seasoning and their deep scorn for the followers of Teflon. These communities involve interests and opinions, but they are also communities with leaders, norms, and boundaries. In short, information breeds interest, but participation breeds socialization.

For politics, this means that digital spaces tend to be geared towards forms of politics rooted in identity and belonging. Digitalization thus intensifies political tribalization by supercharging the rituals that lay the foundation of extremist political movements. While platforms like Stormfront may provide the same emotional and community effects as historical White Power concerts or white-robed gatherings around a burning cross, digital rituals are infinitely more accessible. Simply reaching into your pocket and picking up your phone is enough to join our digital campfire.

The reason for the emphasis on ritualistic forms of politics is that these are powerful in driving user engagement. Rituals are addictive. The emotional energy described by Durkheim and Collins is experienced as a hit of dopamine triggered by receiving a like or a message. Hence, the addictiveness of social media is strongly tied to the formation of social identities. These dynamics are further intensified by the economic logic governing platforms, which seek to maximize attention and engagement. Consequently, large social media platforms seek to support and supercharge the social processes leading to emotional energy. As scholars have argued, social media hence becomes organized around identity-oriented content, emphasizing processes of group belonging (Törnberg & Uitermark, 2022). The addictive designs of social media can be understood as feeding directly into the social rituals that lay the grounds for community formation. In essence, social media is designed for rituals – as these social processes are the most potent mechanisms to stimulate engagement and ensure that users return.

Moreover, the low threshold of participation has meant that online communities come to function as an always-available means of escape: a place of comfort whenever we want to evade loneliness, isolation, or even just boredom. At any given moment, we can reach into our pocket and find ourselves around the campfire with our tribe, our support group, which offers straightforward explanations for what confuses us, excuses for our failures and shortcomings, and convenient scapegoats on whom to lay our blame.

In essence, it is precisely the changes that were once lauded by early internet optimists that have led to a more tribal and polarized political landscape.

What Would Durkheim Say About Counteracting Online Radicalization?

The echo chamber hypothesis is, in many ways, an optimistic theory of online extremism. If extremism is simply a result of a lack of exposure to other perspectives, all that is needed is simply to reach individuals trapped in echo chambers with competing perspectives and arguments. The notion of extreme politics as the accumulation of one-sided arguments suggests that extremists will remain amenable to counterevidence and rational argumentation. The solution thus appears straightforward: we need only to reach them and explain that they are mistaken.

This line of thinking has indeed informed the prevailing approaches to combating online extremism. It has guided interventions to mitigate radicalization and polarization on major platforms like Facebook and Twitter, which have sought to "pop the bubble" by algorithmically promoting diverse interactions across the political spectrum. Similarly, advocacy groups and institutions have pursued a similar strategy, striving to "expose" or "debunk" conspiracy theories by disseminating facts and corrections.

While the Habermasian understanding predicts that such a strategy would be a resounding success, empirical studies have disappointed such expectations. Findings show that exposure to opposing arguments and opinions can, paradoxically, lead those with radical views to become even more extreme. "Debunking" and counter-messaging can similarly exacerbate conflicts and further radicalize individuals who already hold extreme views (Bélanger et al., 2020; Lewandowsky et al., 2012; Törnberg & Wahlström, 2018).

Although these results may confound the Habermasian model of radicalization, they align perfectly with the Durkheimian perspective outlined in this book. So-called echo chambers are not spaces of rational deliberation but rather breeding grounds for collective identity formation. The political narratives that counterarguments seek to "debunk" are, in fact, manifestations of something deeper – something that does not operate in the realm of evidence and arguments. These stories serve as narrative threads that bind individuals to their community, functioning as sacred totems, in Durkheim's terms, and therefore, are not susceptible to rational debate. As discussed in this book, attacks against the community's totem typically yield not introspection and self-questioning but rather impassioned counter-reactions and a rally-around-the-flag dynamic. Once social identities are established, counterarguments and encounters with opposing partisans can instigate identity-based conflict, thereby amplifying radicalization by further unifying the community around a shared enemy (Törnberg, 2022). The Habermasian strategy for deradicalization fails because it does not address the core of radical politics: individuals do not pursue conspiracies or extremist views based on their logical content but for their symbolic meaning and community value.

What strategies and solutions might then a Durkheimian perspective propose for mitigating online radicalization?

The Durkheimian perspective suggests targeting extremism as a community process. Interventions should focus on providing alternative forms of social integration and community support – treating narratives as mere epiphenomena. Individuals who join extreme communities are often dealing with problems in their everyday lives – lack of community, isolation, trauma, or lack of narratives that help them feel connected to a larger community. As we have seen, online communities offer an easily accessible substitute for this sense of social integration, for making sense of an often-confusing world, and for human contact. Conversely, participation in the extreme community often sets off a cycle of further alienation from friends outside the extremist bubble, in turn heightening the dependence on online contact.

Breaking such cycles is not about being proven factually wrong by convincing arguments but is better understood as overcoming an addiction. As we have noted, participation in online rituals creates emotional energy – an addictive rush. Being a well-respected member of an online extremist community offers a sense of importance that one may be lacking in the outside world. Having the ability to navigate the intricate symbolic systems creates an exhilarating feeling of being privy to a secret to which few have access.

Supporting someone we know in leaving extremism is in other words similar to helping them break an addiction. It is emotionally difficult to remain close to someone who is stuck in a toxic worldview, but at the same time, withdrawing from them is likely to make things worse by furthering their isolation. But neither is it constructive to engage with them in discussion by questioning their convictions or disproving their delusions. Much like addressing addiction, it is more effective to reach out to them in a caring and non-judgmental manner – letting them know that you are concerned for their well-being and are willing to support them on their path to recovery.

It may often be more helpful to think of their delusions and stories as pleas for acknowledgment and validation. We need to listen to them – not to the delusions themselves, but to what lies underneath. Their belief in a story of Jews pursuing white genocide may have its roots not in rational arguments, but instead manifest something within their underlying emotional world – their anxieties about a rapidly changing world, feelings of inadequacy, or sense of not belonging. Just as recovery from addiction, leaving online extremism can be a lonely and isolating journey. The best way of supporting such a journey can be to provide emotional support by listening without judgment, being available for them, and encouraging them to stay strong during difficult times. We can seek to guide them towards other campfires around which to gather; healthier communities that fill the same purpose of fostering a sense of belonging and offer the ability to make sense of our often-confusing world.

There are also ways to prevent radicalization from first taking place. To avoid falling into extremism, we can learn to recognize the patterns and pathways through which individuals become immersed in conspiratorial worlds. These are the type of stories that prey on our emotional vulnerabilities, the feeling of community that arises from shared positions, and the desire for something to be true so intensely that critical and rational thinking is sidelined. By familiarizing ourselves with common extremist narratives, we can identify them when we encounter them – and remind ourselves to remain critical. When feeling lonely and disconnected, we can recognize the signs and seek more constructive communities rather than the superficial dopamine of online media. When we feel emotionally triggered by some outrageous opinion that we encounter on social media, we can remind ourselves that these messages are designed and algorithmically enhanced precisely with the purpose of triggering our outrage and generating a reaction – and that they are unlikely to represent any widely held position. We can instead seek content and communities that feed a more inclusive and optimistic view of the world. We can seek to create our digital world in ways that feed not conflict and outrage but the better angels of our nature.

References

Achen, C., & Bartels, L. (2017). *Democracy for realists: Why elections do not produce responsive government*. Princeton, NJ: Princeton University Press.

Bélanger, J. J., Nisa, C. F., Schumpe, B. M., Gurmu, T., Williams, M. J., & Putra, I. E. (2020). Do counter-narratives reduce support for ISIS? Yes, but not for their target audience. *Frontiers in psychology*, 11, 1059.

Lewandowsky, S., Ecker, U. K., Seifert, C. M., Schwarz, N., & Cook, J. (2012). Misinformation and its correction: Continued influence and successful debiasing. *Psychological science in the public interest*, 13(3), 106–131.

Törnberg, A., & Wahlström, M. (2018). Unveiling the radical right online: Exploring framing and identity in an online anti-immigrant discussion group. *Sociologisk forskning*, 55(2–3), 267–292.

Törnberg, P. (2022). How digital media drive affective polarization through partisan sorting. *PNAS*, 119(42). 1–11.

Törnberg, P., Andersson, C., Lindgren, K., & Banisch, S. (2021). Modeling the emergence of affective polarization in the social media society. *PloS one*, 16(10), e0258259.

Törnberg, P., & Uitermark, J. (2022). Tweeting ourselves to death: The cultural logic of digital capitalism. *Media, culture & society*, 44(3), 574–590.

Wintemute, G. J., Robinson, S., Crawford, A., Schleimer, J. P., Barnhorst, A., Chaplin, V., … Pear, V. A. (2022). Views of American democracy and society and support for political violence: First report from a nationwide population-representative survey. *medRxiv* 2022.2007. 2015.22277693. https://doi.org/10.1101/2022.07.15.22277693

Epilogue

Forty years after his failed invasion of Dominica, Don Black became part of yet another attempt to overthrow a democratically elected government. But this time, the intended victim was not a small island nation.

Don Black's prison programming course in the 1990s had been more impactful than he could have imagined. It would be part of a technological media transformation that would, over the next decades, transform politics and bring about a wave of far-right political movements.

Stormfront would provide a safe meeting space for a growing number of individuals who shared a feeling of discomfort about the current politics – who had experienced the recent decades of progress on minority rights as decades of their own retreat. The election of Obama in 2008, in particular, became a symbol of their loss. Someone who, a mere generation earlier, would not have been allowed into a movie theatre claimed the highest post in the nation. For some white Americans, this was deeply unsettling – things being *out of place* – a threat against something unspoken at the very core of how they understood themselves. The event was less understood than viscerally *felt.*

Stormfront gave these white Americans a safe space where they could gather, feel that they were not alone, and tentatively seek to articulate what had previously been merely an unspoken discomfort. *Hussein Obama doesn't know his place.* An articular that simultaneously transformed the amorphous group of white Americans into something more like an intimate community. Make sense of themselves, the world, and the relationship between the two. *We, white people, are superior.* To respond to threats to their identity, that something perturbed in the natural order of things. *We have become a repressed majority.* A construction of a social identity that was entangled with the construction of an internal discourse and culture, blurring the line between internal identity-building and socialization. *We are the ones who resist.* These stories, at the same time, guided and directed their actions and gave them a purpose. It transformed disappointment and fear into anger and outrage. *We need to fight back.* It transformed anger and outrage into a decision to act. *The time for talk is over.*

On January 6, 2021, 40 years after Don Black's arrest, that anger was transformed into action as the wave of far-right extremism that had been building for decades broke with full force into the US Capitol. The mob sought to overthrow not merely the government of a small Caribbean Island but of the United States. Armed and prepared to take hostages, the mob came mere meters from reaching their intended victims: the US Senators and Vice President.

While unprecedented, the event was in many ways typical and emblematic of the pattern of political movements spawned on and through digital spaces such as Stormfront. The mob was fueled by misinformation, energized by shared outrage, and driven by a sense of common purpose. The storming was, in many ways, just another expression of a growing trend of digital extremists leaving their hiding places in fringe digital spaces to violently burst upon the political scene.

Just like Don Black's dream of making Dominica a white neo-Nazi state in 1981, the January 6th uprising failed. But just as the arrest of Don Black proved a pyrrhic victory for progressive forces, so may the failure of the January 6th insurrection prove expressive of just how successful Don Black had been in his ambitions.

Many of the ideas of Don Black are no longer merely part of the fringe extreme but have entered into the political mainstream. Social media have brought a shift in cultural hegemony. The simmering white resentment that had previously been subterranean had now surfaced, bringing racial and cultural conflicts into the light of day.

While Stormfront has fallen in importance in recent years, it has been supplanted by new and ever-growing digital spaces: Dailystormer, Gab, Voat, and 4chan. Sites that are controlled and governed by private individuals, who set their own rules of interaction and create their own cultural hegemonies in their own private thiefdoms.

Through the invasion of Dominica, Don Black had wanted to create a safe space for neo-Nazis. A space where they could meet and mobilize outside of reach of the government. A space from which they could launch their attacks.

But for this aim, he did not need to overthrow a government. Today, we can all enter into Don Black's neo-Nazi state by simply reaching into our pocket.

We have yet to see the full implications of this possibility on our politics, as the online, in turn, tends to reach back into our offline world. As a user on Stormfront called on January 6th, 2021: "Enough talk. I love Stormfront but the time for talk is over. Time to fight."

Index

For Product Safety Concerns and Information please contact our EU
representative GPSR@taylorandfrancis.com
Taylor & Francis Verlag GmbH, Kaufingerstraße 24, 80331 München, Germany